VOLUNTARY AID FOR DEVELOPMENT
The role of Non-Governmental Organisations

ORGANISATION FOR ECONOMIC CO-OPERATION AND DEVELOPMENT

Pursuant to article 1 of the Convention signed in Paris on 14th December, 1960, and which came into force on 30th September, 1961, the Organisation for Economic Co-operation and Development (OECD) shall promote policies designed:

- to achieve the highest sustainable economic growth and employment and a rising standard of living in Member countries, while maintaining financial stability, and thus to contribute to the development of the world economy;
- to contribute to sound economic expansion in Member as well as non-member countries in the process of economic development; and
- to contribute to the expansion of world trade on a multilateral, non-discriminatory basis in accordance with international obligations.

The original Member countries of the OECD are Austria, Belgium, Canada, Denmark, France, the Federal Republic of Germany, Greece, Iceland, Ireland, Italy, Luxembourg, the Netherlands, Norway, Portugal, Spain, Sweden, Switzerland, Turkey, the United Kingdom and the United States. The following countries acceded subsequently through accession at the dates hereafter: Japan (28th April, 1964), Finland (28th January, 1969), Australia (7th June, 1971) and New Zealand (29th May, 1973).

The Socialist Federal Republic of Yugoslavia takes part in some of the work of the OECD (agreement of 28th October, 1961).

Publié en français sous le titre:

DES PARTENAIRES DANS L'ACTION
POUR LE DÉVELOPPEMENT :
Les organisations
non gouvernementales

This survey has been compiled by
the OECD Development Co-operation Directorate
and is published on the responsibility
of the Secretary-General

Also Available

FINANCING AND EXTERNAL DEBT OF DEVELOPING COUNTRIES. 1987 SURVEY (July 1988)
(43 88 04 1) ISBN 92-64-13095-0   224 pages   £13.00   US$24.50   F110.00   DM48.00

EVALUATION IN DEVELOPING COUNTRIES: A step in a Dialogue (May 1988)
(43 88 03 1) ISBN 92-64-123071-3   56 pages   £7.00   US$13.50   F60.00   DM26.00

IN-SERVICE TRAINING AND THE DEVELOPMENT OF HUMAN RESOUR-CES: Five Asian Experiences by Bernard Salomé and Jacques Charmes (May 1988)
(41 88 02 1) ISBN 92-63-13077-2   78 pages   £7.00   US$13.50   F60.00   DM26.00

DEVELOPING COUNTRIES DEBT: THE BUDGETARY AND TRANSFER PRO-BLEM by Helmut Reisen and Axel Van Trotsenburg (March 1988)
(41 88 01 1) ISBN 92-64-13053-5   196 pages   £14.00   US$26.40   F120.00   DM52.00

DEVELOPMENT POLICIES AND THE CRISIS OF THE 1980s (August 1987)
(41 87 03 1) ISBN 92-64-12992-8   178 pages   £11.00   US$23.00   F110.00   DM47.00

* * *

DEVELOPMENT CO-OPERATION. 1988 REPORT (To be published in December 1988)

FOREWORD

by
Mr. Joseph C. Wheeler
Chairman of the DAC
(Development Assistance Committee of the OECD)

For generations solidarity with people in other parts of the world has been expressed through individual and group activities supporting schools, hospitals and other activities. Today we call this "development". Private groups have long histories of service and today's public and private agencies owe a great deal to those pioneering efforts. They taught us to care.

Forty years ago there began a new era. Many new countries acceded to independence and public programmes of assistance were begun or expanded. Our view has become increasingly global and our horizons have extended. People's response to Africa's recent drought was a dramatic demonstration of the concern they have come to have for the problems of others.

The voluntary sector has frequently articulated new policy insights reflecting changes which have been taking place in our societies. Ask an aid administrator why he or she has increased the emphasis on environmental concerns -- or women in development, or population. Ask where the pressure comes from for more emphasis on reaching the poor, or on health and education. The answer is that these are concerns of our populations expressed through our political processes and usually pointed up by what we call our non-governmental organisations.

But this dialogue works both ways. Official agencies are recognising that development is an enabling process -- not primarily a welfare programme. They have encouraged the NGO community to go further in that direction and the NGOs have responded.

In the Development Assistance Committee -- the OECD Committee in which we seek consensus on aid matters -- we have come to recognise the mutually supporting roles among official and non-official organisations. To us on the official side the NGO sector represents an educator of our publics, an aspect of our support, the origin of some of our policy, a welcome financial contribution, the source of insights on methodology and a vehicle for administering a portion of our official assistance.

Today the DAC-country NGOs raise from their constituencies approximately $3 billion for developmental activities in the developing countries. Our aid agencies channel another $1.5 billion through these organisations. Attention is shifting in response to changing circumstances and new insights. For example, there is increasing respect for the growing role of local groups in developing countries. There is increasing interest in the policy framework as it affects project success. We note the willingness of more NGOs to plan their activities over a longer period -- to stay with programmes and to emphasize sustainability. We also see a shift toward job creation. These are things we are moving on together.

The NGO community flourishes in its independence and our views are not likely to be identical. But at bottom we know that the NGOs and the official aid agencies can learn from each other and that there is considerable common ground. Thus DAC will continue to be interested in what NGOs do and how we can help each other.

This report reflects recent discussion in the DAC on the role of non-governmental organisations. We plan another meeting in 1988. I am sure that this report will provide useful background for our continuing exchange of views.

We can all be grateful to the OECD Secretariat for its prodigious work leading up to this report. It is published with financial support from the Government of the Netherlands.

Joseph C. Wheeler

TABLE OF CONTENTS

INTRODUCTION

Members of the Development Assistance Committee (DAC) of the Organisation for Economic Co-operation and Development (OECD) have shown an increasing interest in recent years in the activities of non-governmental organisations (NGOs) and their contribution to development.

NGOs are well known for their active role in emergencies, attracting attention to desperate situations, raising funds and organising relief. Their help during the African famine of 1984-85 won widespread recognition. This is only one aspect of their work, however, and it should not obscure their growing importance in the difficult business of promoting economic and social development in the poorest countries over the longer term.

By 1985, the annual amount of grants to developing countries by private voluntary agencies amounted to $2.89 billion, the equivalent of 10 per cent of total official development assistance (ODA) from DAC Members that year. In addition, about 5 per cent of ODA from DAC Members taken together is channelled through NGOs (see Table 1 in Chapter IV). Individual country shares vary widely, but all Members of DAC have had mechanisms for cofinancing activities of NGOs in developing countries for more than a decade -- some for much longer. In most DAC countries, these were later followed by similar arrangements, albeit generally on a modest scale, for the cofinancing of information activities addressed to the public in Member countries ("development education"). More recently, the official aid agencies of some Member countries have also started providing direct funding for NGOs of developing countries ("NGOs of the South").

Since the early 1980s in evaluations conducted by official aid agencies, much attention has been paid to NGOs' specific characteristics and comparative advantage as "development agencies". Currently, their role in strengthening partner institutions in developing countries, particularly local self-help organisations, is acquiring prominence in research. This is a recognition of the potential of local self-help NGOs in poverty-alleviation programmes. The African famine of 1984-85 reinforced the interest in NGOs' partnership with self-help groups such as village and small farmers' associations in developing countries. It also gave rise to a feeling of urgency concerning the need for coherence and the search for complementarities between official and private developmental efforts. One of the reasons for stressing complementarities is that both private and official agencies are faced with highly complex and difficult tasks as, indeed, are developing countries themselves. Some of the difficulties are common, others are specific to the NGO sector with its generally smaller scale of activities and often uncertainty as to the resources it can raise.

It is against this background that the DAC held a meeting with NGOs in February 1985 on collaboration between official aid agencies and NGOs. This was followed in June 1986 by a seminar on the role of NGOs in agricultural and rural development in Sub-Saharan Africa. Members asked the Secretariat to prepare a report to make the information collected in relation to NGO activities available to a wider public. The government of the Netherlands further contributed a grant to the OECD for the publication of the report.

The report is thematic. A historical approach is followed in presenting NGOs of Member countries and their evolution in developmental matters up to the present day (Chapter I). The aim is to identify trends rather than to describe the NGO community in individual Member countries in sequence. As is appropriate for a study by the Secretariat of the OECD, much attention is paid to co-operation between official aid agencies and NGOs.

NGOs of developing countries are discussed with an emphasis on the particular types of organisation which interest most OECD Members' official and private developmental agencies: self-help groups at the grass-roots level and their federations; institutions and organisations in developing countries which actively promote and support self-help groups through the provision of training, technical assistance, credit etc.; consultative NGO councils within host countries (Chapter II). Illustrations for this chapter are drawn from experience in Sub-Saharan Africa.

Issues of central interest when considering NGOs' developmental activities include replicability, institution-building, impact, the links between the "micro" level at which they usually operate and broader development policies, and types of evaluation most suited to partner NGOs in developing countries. Drawing on recent research and on illustrations from relevant experience mainly in Asia, these issues are reviewed in Chapter III. The chapter further provides information and findings from research and experience on other issues of current interest such as NGOs' role in the promotion of small enterprise and appropriate technology, the advocacy by NGOs of "triangular operations" to respond to food requirements in some African countries, and new financial tools that are being evolved by NGOs.

Different arrangements have been worked out by some DAC Members to institutionalise a dialogue with NGOs and by all Members for co-funding of NGO developmental activities (Chapter IV). Adjustments are being made to increase flexibility, through greater reliance on "block grants" for example, and more exceptionally by providing non-earmarked credit lines to mature partner groups in the field or direct funding to domestic NGOs of developing countries. Various arrangements for co-operating with NGOs have also been established by agencies within the United Nations system, the World Bank and more recently the Asian Development Bank.

A considerable body of evaluations has built up over this decade, particularly by Member countries' aid agencies wishing to assess the performance of NGOs as development agencies and the adequacy of current programmes and arrangements for public sector co-operation with them. The evidence and recommendations from available evaluations are summarised in Chapter V.

In addition to publicity for fund-raising, NGOs are increasingly involved in providing broader information to the public, through development education activities (Chapter VI). These often encompass aid within a wider framework of North-South interdependence. NGOs are recognised as having a major impact in generating support for aid and for keeping development issues before the public as well as parliaments.

Where does all this take NGOs today? A watershed conference convened in London by the World Development journal of Washington and London's Overseas Development Institute in March 1987 (see Chapter I) threw light on current interaction between NGOs of the North (including in this context, of course, Australia and New Zealand) and their partners in the South, implying a redefinition of roles and a broader mandate to NGOs of the North in advocacy of developmental issues. The articulation between local-level, relatively small NGO operations in the field and the broader policy contexts, especially at sub-national level, is another issue currently on the agenda. Closer interaction between the private voluntary and the public sector may be required to enhance complementarities in the interest of the ultimate beneficiary population groups. Some of these challenges and their implications are touched upon in the Conclusions.

Annexes include a list of abbreviations, a statement prepared by NGOs which were represented at the DAC seminar held in June 1986, indicators recently elaborated by researchers for assessing institutional development, and statistical tables.

Chapter I

NGOs OF DAC MEMBER COUNTRIES

There is much interest nowadays in NGOs as "development agencies", yet there is wide recognition of their special nature and their autonomy. What makes NGOs special can best be gathered by looking at their origins: many did not start as development agencies at all. They were often drawn to development by first providing relief in emergency situations, and by coming to recognise that in developing countries relief was not enough. Financial support from DAC Member countries' governments sustained the developmental element in the NGO sector. Yet, many of them remain tributary to their home constituencies for fund-raising, hence, the often relatively small size of their operations. This triangular relation, to people in the home and the host countries, and to governments, together with their historic evolution and their commitment to the poor, does give NGOs distinctive features as compared with other actors in development co-operation.

Definitions of NGOs

A voluntary agency is an organisation established and governed by a group of private citizens for a stated philanthropic purpose, and supported by voluntary individual contributions. The broader usage, "non-profit organisation", encompasses most of the voluntary organisations. An even broader term is "non-governmental organisation" or "NGO". This term is often used almost interchangeably with "voluntary agency", although the term "NGO" may include profit-making organisations, foundations, educational institutions, churches and other religious groups and missions, medical organisations and hospitals, unions and professional organisations, business and commercial associations, co-operatives and cultural groups, as well as voluntary agencies. Defining voluntary agencies and non-governmental organisations further depends upon the particular situation within a given country. The definition given here is taken from Councils for Development, TAICH/ACVAFS and IADS (Washington DC, 1981).

The term "NGO" has acquired wide acceptance internationally. "Private voluntary organisation" or PVO is the term most commonly used in the United States. Third World agencies seem, however, to be moving consciously away from the term "NGO", with the terms "non-governmental development organisations" used in South America, and "voluntary development organisations" used by African NGOs in Sub-Saharan Africa in recent years.

An important distinction should be made between non-governmental agencies whose main purpose is related to developing countries (whether for development or relief), and those which include developmental or developing-country concerns but also have other purposes. Examples of the latter include missions and religious orders, part of whose activities are of an ecclesiastical nature, while other activities provide social services (health, education) and fund development projects. The Ford and Rockefeller Foundations could also be considered as part of this group, as they operate both in the United States and in developing countries.

Developmental NGOs

One of the main features of NGOs that seek to provide aid in one form or another is their great diversity. A number of them are partly, and in some cases even wholly, financed by governments, but most of them must raise the bulk of their funds from the public.

The brief characterisation of relief and developmental NGOs sketched by Sir Geoffrey Wilson in 1981 still provides a good picture. [Sir Geoffrey Wilson, Chairman of Oxfam, "The role of non-governmental organisations in aid to the least-developed countries", in The Role of Non-Governmental Organisations in Development Co-operation, Liaison Bulletin between Development Research and Training Institutes, No 10, Development Centre OECD, 1983.]

Most are concerned with development -- agricultural, social, medical, educational, etc. -- in both urban and rural environments. Some are highly specialised and serviced by highly specialised staffs. Of the wide variety of organisations operating internationally, church-related bodies still make up the largest number. The Red Cross societies, refugee relief bodies, the International Planned Parenthood Federation and its affiliated members, and Save the Children Fund organisations account for another "group" of specialised NGOs; followed by the specialist organisations concerned with leprosy, the blind, and other particular professional fields like adult literacy, agricultural development and vocational training. The remainder consist of private foundations like Rockefeller and Ford, which provide funding; organisations like OXFAM, which support a wide range of activities; some "half-and-half" organisations that receive considerable government funding; such as CARE and the volunteer-sending agencies; and a larger number of small groups that fall into none of the above categories.

A primary difference between NGOs and bilateral and multilateral government organisations is that NGOs are at the other end of the scale in terms of size. Except where they are financed by governments, their dependence on voluntary donations keep them small, by itself a pressure to do more with fewer resources. This means that NGOs can and must work with local groups and individuals: the competence and commitment, success or failure of these groups and individuals determines their own success or failure.

Developmental NGOs in a broader national associative context

NGOs are a feature of many cultures and societies. In western countries, those which deal with development or development education constitute only a fraction of the national voluntary organisations. (Sources used for data on individual countries and for other background data are identified in footnotes at the end of the chapter, while publications cited at greater length are mentioned in the body of the text.) In Canada, 40 000 registered charities were reported in 1980, of which perhaps about 220 were exclusively concerned with international development [Tim Brodhead and Brent Herbert-Copley with Anne-Marie Lambert, Research Associate, Bridges of Hope? Canadian Voluntary Agencies and the Third World, the North-South Institute, Ottawa, 1988]. In Sweden, NGOs, the largest of which are often referred to as "folkrörelser" (popular movements), have a long tradition in the field of development. They include trade unions, co-operatives, the churches and a wide range of non-profit associations. Even in small Swedish municipalities of 5 000 to 10 000 inhabitants, approximately one hundred NGOs are recorded in all sorts of activities. Over the twenty years up to the early 1980s, approximately 200 NGOs had undertaken developmental activities with cofinancing by SIDA (1). In Finland, there are few organisations specialising in development co-operation, rather, a number of existing ones such as youth movements, friendship societies, women's organisations, trade unions, churches etc. have gradually added development to their traditional activities. In the United States just under 500 PVOs were listed in 1983 as being concerned with development assistance abroad (2). By comparison, a total of some 300 000 agencies and associations raise funds from the American public ($53.6 billion in 1981) for mainly domestic philanthropic purposes (3). In the United Kingdom, there are approximately one million volunteers, offering time to work unpaid in hospitals, old people's homes, etc., while approximately 1 650 volunteers served overseas in 1985. Approximately one hundred British NGOs are mainly development-oriented, in a total of approximately 150 000 registered British charities including many smaller ones (4).

The specific country contexts in which NGOs are rooted have implications for their "philosophy" and the historical experience on which they draw, for example in social work. Developmental NGOs face competition from other charities in fund-raising. The need to maximise their fund-raising potential may affect the content of their overseas programmes.

Some considerations on numbers and size of NGOs

Precise data on numbers of developmental NGOs in DAC countries are not available. There are many more than are registered with the official aid agencies in countries which practise such registration, and many more than the 1 702 listed in the last comprehensive directory covering OECD Member countries published by the OECD Development Centre in 1981 (5). Indeed, the Development Centre is now preparing an up-dated directory on the basis of a list of over 4 000 NGOs (publication foreseen for 1989). For France alone, the latest directory lists 520 NGOs (6), and in Japan, a country where until recently NGOs were in a formative stage, 131 NGOs and foundations were listed in 1985 (7) and 257 in 1986.

In most DAC countries, however, the bulk of fund-raising and overseas activities is accounted for by a small number of relatively large NGOs. There may be hundreds of smaller ones, of local rather than national scale, not taking into account the countless ephemeral groups. In Canada, 316 NGOs were listed by the Canadian Council for International Co-operation in 1986 and 114 of these provided financial data: 30 showed an income from private sources of over C$ 1 million (fifteen of these were church-related), and only three of over C$ 10 million (8). Of the 167 PVOs registered with US AID in 1983, 14 accounted for 81 per cent of total cash private contributions ($719 million)

16

donated to registered PVOs as a whole (9). Altogether, an experienced NGO professional recently estimated that approximately 200 developmental NGOs in DAC countries combined may account for some three-fourths of their total grants to developing countries (10).

The number and size of NGOs certainly has relevance for cofinancing procedures and the processing of requests for aid agencies' funding (see Chapter IV). Conversely, when the accompanying administrative requirements are complex, official grants are much more exacting on the time and staff of individual NGOs. Agency size also determines the amount of time and staff which NGOs can devote to development education as distinct from fund-raising activities, their capacity to carry out evaluations, etc.

The existence of many smaller groups is a reason for favouring and supporting linking arrangements. For example, a number of smaller autonomous NGOs in the French provinces have joined to establish a single secretariat in Paris for liaison with the "collectifs" (umbrella organisations) formed by French NGOs over the past few years, and with governmental services.

Size, however, is not the only issue. The variety of dimension, purpose, origin and inspiration which is a major feature of the NGO community is also one of its strengths. The specialisation and quality of know-how transfers effected by some relatively small NGOs may give them an invaluable role in specific sectors. This was found to be the case for some US PVOs (such as the Credit Union National Association, the International Executive Service Corps, and the Institute for International Development), which draw on the expertise of active and retired businessmen and managers, to provide essential technical service and resources for small groups of entrepreneurs in developing countries (11). Indeed, DAC Members' official aid agencies recognise the relatively small scale of NGOs and their activities as one of their comparative advantages.

But there are more intrinsic reasons for not giving exclusive attention to size. NGOs are private associations, and as such represent the concern of groups of citizens in OECD countries. NGOs would exist even were there no financial contributions from governments; indeed, many started before the establishment of such co-operative arrangements. Nor do they all have the ambition of growing into large organisations. Many pursue goals in relief, development or advocacy which are important, irrespective of scale, and have in some cases been at the origin of widespread change or contributed to it. Smaller groups may also perform a valuable role in creating links between DAC countries and developing countries, by nurturing a deeper awareness and feeling for global interdependence in public opinion at the level of local communities.

An assessment of NGOs' activities requires an understanding of the autonomy and variety of their goals, values and styles. A historic sketch of NGOs, their involvement with developing countries and their relations with the official development co-operation agencies, with examples of how some significant agencies or activities grew to be what they are now, is attempted in the following sections of this chapter.

Origins of development-oriented NGOs

In many DAC countries, NGOs as they are currently known have two cultural matrixes. One, the very concept on which they operate, "freedom of association", emerged in the nineteenth century from the rise to prominence of the western bourgeoisie, and the liberal democratic values they professed (12). The British and Foreign Anti-Slavery Society, established in 1823 and still active, is an early prototype of the modern NGO derived from this source.

The second, more specifically overseas-oriented base is represented by Catholic and Protestant missions and their work in the education and health sectors, especially in Africa and Asia, starting mainly in the nineteenth century. Indeed, church-linked and other agencies of religious inspiration figure prominently among NGOs today (13). For example in Germany -- the European country with the largest private donations and official contributions to NGOs -- the resources for developmental purposes of Protestant agencies, in 1986, amounted to $214 million, of Catholic agencies to $189 million and of non-denominational groups to $142 million. This does not include contributions to NGOs from the official aid sector.

First steps in relief: the post-war experience

In a number of DAC countries, a first generation of NGOs started after the First World War (examples include the Caritas agencies in a number of countries and the Near East Foundation in the United States) and gathered new strength at the end of the Second World War, with much of the focus on relief and rehabilitation in the devastated European countries. In the United States, NGOs involved in planning aid to Europe established an American Council of Private Foreign Relief Agencies as early as October 1943. In the immediate post-war years, US NGOs were heavily involved in helping European populations, refugees and displaced persons with clothing, food, and medical supplies, both on privately raised funds and helping distribute US government aid. Two of the largest US PVOs were founded for this purpose: Catholic Relief Services (CRS) in 1943, and CARE (Co-operative for American Relief Everywhere), established by 23 agencies in 1945. Up to mid-1946, the major effort was to prevent famine in Europe.

In the United Kingdom, the Oxford Committee for Famine Relief was started in October 1942 by a half-dozen people including the mayor of Oxford (a Quaker), the vicar of the University Church and a specialist in Greek literature. Their first concern was to bring relief to starving civilians in Nazi-occupied Greece. Their committee developed into Oxfam, the largest British developmental NGO today. A similar impetus for post-war reconstruction led to the start of Christian Aid. The Save the Children Fund, the oldest of the large British foreign aid charities, was founded in 1919, from the Fight the Famine Council which opposed the Allied blockade of Germany (14).

Likewise, in Denmark, the Danish Association for International Co-operation ("Mellenfolkeligt Samwirke"), a major lay NGO, was founded in 1944 under the name of "Friends of Peace Relief Work". In the immediate post-war years it enabled hundreds of young Danes to travel to Western and Eastern European countries and Israel to help reconstruct what the war had destroyed.

Other emergency situations calling for immediate relief continued to break out, many of them in developing countries, such as the uprooting of 17 million people following the partitioning of India in 1947, the flight of 800 000 Arab refugees from Palestine in 1948, the migration of over 4 million people over the years after the victory of the Communist forces in China in 1949, the Korean war in 1950, starvation in Bihar in 1951... the catalogue continued decade after decade. Many of the NGOs which started as relief agencies with a focus on Europe subsequently responded to these new emergencies in other parts of the world.

Gradually, a number of NGOs also became involved in work of a developmental nature as their horizon widened and as they perceived that in these parts of the world emergencies were often only the tip of an iceberg of chronic deprivation.

From relief to development

Significant points in the evolution of NGOs towards developmental concerns were the accession of many countries to independence in the early 1960s, the change in relationships between churches in developed and developing countries which followed these political changes and the launching by FAO of the Freedom from Hunger Campaign in 1960.

In Sweden, a turning point was the accession to independence of many countries in Asia. With the initial design of supporting democracy in these countries, 44 national-level associations such as trade unions, co-operative unions and religious organisations formed a committee in 1952 to handle public funds for developmental purposes. The first projects were in Ethiopia and Pakistan. From the start this committee was concerned with building up public support in Sweden for development assistance.

In the United States, early steps included President Truman's "Point IV" proclaimed in January 1949 to extend US efforts "for the improvement and growth of underdeveloped areas", and the Agricultural Act of the same year. Under Point IV, American voluntary agencies started receiving modest official grants as from 1951, for technical assistance and developmental work in the Near East, Cameroon, India, Israel. Under the Agricultural Act of 1949 (section 416), which with the subsequent Public Law 480 of 1954 still provides the legislative framework of food aid, voluntary agencies also qualified for the distribution of surplus food stocks to people in need in countries overseas. The distribution of food aid still remains the major function of two giant American PVOs: CARE (total resources including governmental sources: $274 million in 1985, of which 87 per cent for food aid including freight) and CRS (total resources: $437 million in 1985, of which over 80 per cent for food aid) (15). In addition to relief, they design and manage nutrition programmes and food for work projects, e.g., for major rural developmental/poverty alleviation activities such as road construction, water schemes, etc. (16).

The churches and NGOs of religious inspiration

The churches were innovators in the late 1960s in promoting the concept of "partners" in developing countries. Their first partners were the national churches overseas, which in many countries were reshaped following independence, implying changes in relationships with sister churches in the industrialised countries (17). Churches were the originators, and, by virtue of the universality of their constituencies, powerful vehicles of many of the values shared today by a large section of the NGO community. For example, the encyclical letters Pacem in Terris (1963) and Populorum Progressio (1967) of Popes John XXIII and Paul VI established the principle that human beings are the agents and goals of development and enunciated principles of self-reliance and international solidarity. These documents listed the "legitimate aspirations" of populations in developing and newly independent countries: freedom from poverty, greater assurance of finding their sustenance, health, stable employment, more responsibility, freedom from all oppression, more education, and, in newly independent countries, autonomous growth and dignity, both economic and social, in addition to the political freedom represented by independence. They also underlined the "scandal of crying inequalities" in the sharing of goods and of power. In 1958, the World Council of Churches recommended for the first time the target of 1 per cent of industrial countries' national income for financial transfers to developing countries, a target which was later to be adopted in the framework of the United Nations and to evolve into the more specific target of 0.7 per cent for official development assistance. Protestant churches were invited by the World Council of Churches from 1968 onwards to devote a share of their resources (later specified at 2 per cent) to development aid -- over and above their aid for developing countries' churches themselves. Sharing was instituted "not as a remedy but as a form of education". In 1981, for example, 416 of the 1 160 parishes of the Dutch Reformed Church devoted 2 per cent of their resources to development aid.

The vast majority of church-related NGOs distinguish their religious from their developmental activities and exclude proselytising from the latter. There are some exceptions, which seem to be confined to a few instances of minor denominations, in emergency situations such as aid to refugees and otherwise. Although regrettable, these remain exceptions. To maintain the distinction, major denominations have established a double network of agencies. One is of an interchurch nature, including relief, welfare and development aid under the aegis of the churches, within an ecclesiastical mainstream which is not limited to developing countries. The second network, while based on church constituencies in the donor countries, is made up of lay agencies which focus on the developing countries and their relief and developmental requirements, often in partnership with partner groups of the same denomination (18). In the Catholic Church, the respective international networks are Caritas Internationalis and Coopération internationale pour le développement et la solidarité (CIDSE). In 1988, CIDSE grouped 14 developmental NGOs from 11 OECD countries in Europe and North America. The resources of these affiliates totalled around $330 million including as well funds raised privately and through cofinancing. They support more than 6 000 projects annually, proposed by partners in the Third World. All CIDSE members are also involved in a wide range of development education activities and lobbying on major issues such as Third World debt. In the World Council of Churches, a similar distinction is drawn between two different committees: one dealing with interchurch aid, the other with the participation of churches in development. Even when the aid is ecclesiastical and channelled through a local church, the dialogue among the faithful nowadays appears to bear on broadening the perception of who the intended beneficiaries should be, from one based on the community of faith to one encompassing the local community as a whole. (But developments along these lines are not linear in all cases: for an illustration of local partner institutions deciding to narrow their role to serving community members within an ecclesiastical divide, see An evaluation of the CEBEMO Programme in the Philippines, 1980-1983, No 21 in the series of programme evaluations of the Dutch cofinancing development programme, The Hague, 1985.)

In countless instances, missions and agencies of religious inspiration develop their social and developmental activities to the benefit of the local population regardless of creed. They provide essential health care, education and training, material and technical assistance for agriculture, etc., in deprived areas, in particular in Sub-Saharan Africa. The rural development project of Podor in Senegal, supported by a German Protestant developmental NGO (EZE) in a Muslim area, and with a Muslim director, epitomises this broader concept of partnership.

Freedom from hunger, micro-projects and volunteers in the 1960s

The FAO Freedom from Hunger Campaign launched in 1960 chose as its motto the ancient oriental proverb: "Give a man a fish, and you feed him for a day; teach him to fish, and you feed him for a lifetime." National "freedom from hunger" associations were established in a number of DAC countries to foster the aims of the campaign. Some of these are important to this day, for example the Comité français contre la faim (CFCF), founded in 1960 and grouping 60 French organisations, or Deutsche Welthungerhilfe in Germany (1963).

Technical assistance and developmental activities of many denominational and secular NGOs in the 1960s were often of a very small scale ("micro-projects", "microréalisations"). A concern with training of local talent also grew in the early 1960s and led to the establishment by some religious and lay NGOs of permanent training centres in developing countries. In Sub-Saharan Africa, several were of a regional character, covering more than one country. To this day they serve educational and training needs of rural populations and other categories, through a diversified range of group courses for villagers (men and women), correspondence courses, etc. This institution-building activity and the training imparted helped prepare the ground for the emergence some 15-20 years later of local self-help groups in the countries concerned.

Other features of a number of developmental NGOs of the 1960s and early 1970s included an extensive use of young and often inexperienced volunteers and the perception of NGOs' role as "achievers" or direct "providers" of services, not yet as catalysts to local efforts. The "achiever" trait was strengthened by the introduction of matching grants by governmental agencies in some DAC countries. In most cases the official contribution was extended on the basis of an approved "project" with precise indications on expected inputs, and of planned outputs which were often expressed in "bricks-and-mortar" terms.

In some DAC countries, certain NGOs specialised in the provision of volunteers. Over the years, these agencies gradually became more demanding in terms of the qualifications and experience required of candidates. Indeed the personnel some of them supply nowadays is highly qualified and assigned to demanding tasks. Some of these specialised volunteer agencies are mainly or even fully supported by official funds, for example Voluntary Service Overseas (VSO) in the United Kingdom and the Association française des volontaires du progrès (AFVP) in France. In Italy the concept of NGOs was virtually limited to the provision of volunteers until recently, and a broader perception of NGOs' potential for contributing to development started evolving only in the past few years.

Together with the official volunteer corps established by several DAC Members (such as the Peace Corps created by President John Kennedy in 1961), private volunteer agencies enabled tens of thousands of citizens of DAC countries to acquire first-hand experience of developing-country situations and sensitivity to global issues. By 1985, the Peace Corps alone had fielded 25 000 volunteers. Returned volunteers represent an important source of recruitment for other official and non-governmental development-related agencies, and are a resource for development education in their countries of origin. A recent Canadian study suggests that with increased professionalism there are now fewer opportunities for ordinary citizens to volunteer their work for NGOs whether at home or overseas, entailing a loss of opportunity for education to international issues. NGOs should develop strategies to reverse this trend and encourage the participation of ordinary citizens in some of their work (Bridges of Hope? op. cit.).

Not all NGOs, however, perceived themselves as "achievers". Some saw their role very early on mainly as one of providing -- even on a very small scale -- the missing piece of equipment or the initial fund to start a system of revolving loans which a local initiative needed to succeed, rather than themselves implementing a project in the field. A pioneering path in this respect was followed by Oxfam from 1961, when it posted its first "field director" in Africa. Oxfam chose from the start not to implement projects itself but fund small local initiatives through small grants (still averaging only £1 000 each in the early 1980s), although it provides on occasion sizeable amounts for emergencies and development. By the end of 1987, Oxfam's field offices numbered 35, covering approximately 70 countries. With prolonged experience and familiarity with local communities and groups, field directors also gradually acquire an expertise in rural development that enables them to identify and stimulate promising initiatives. For example, the discernment of Oxfam in devoting an exceptionally high share of its health aid to primary health care as from the early 1970s has been ascribed in part to the experience and active stance of its field directors. [See Susan Cole-King, "Primary Health Care and the Role of Foreign Aid", in Two Papers on Health Aid, IDS Communication 123, Institute of Development Studies, University of Sussex, 1979.] Experience showed that responding to locally initiated requests was not enough if the agency wished to reach the poorest of the poor: articulating a request for assistance is often beyond their capabilities. The functions of field directors thus include the identification of smaller specially deprived groups in areas of the country not assisted by other agencies. And, once small community groups are identified, the experience of field directors is that they can realistically absorb only quite small amounts of funds. It may look questionable from a purely cost-effective standpoint for a field director to travel several thousands of miles yearly searching out tiny projects. The answer lies with the "philosophy" of the agency, which seeks opportunities for providing grants as catalytic inputs to processes which it sees as being the responsibility of local groups. In fact, grants from Oxfam frequently figure among lists of early donors to groups which later became significant NGOs within developing countries.

Relief activities continued to be needed as disasters, both natural and man-made, unfolded. A number of NGOs involved in developmental work thus maintained a relief component. Emergencies such as the Nigerian civil war and the Biafra famine (1967-70) were also the starting point of new specialised NGOs, such as the French Médecins sans frontières, established in 1971 and highly specialised in medical emergency assistance (19).

An event in international liaison among NGOs was the creation in 1962 of the International Council of Voluntary Agencies (ICVA) from the merger of consultative groups among NGOs concerned with refugees and displaced persons. To this day ICVA, together with the EEC/NGO Liaison Committee, is one of the two most significant non-denominational permanent structures for consultation among NGOs internationally. In 1987 it counted over 80 secular as well as denominational member agencies. In addition to DAC Member countries' and international NGOs, ICVA's affiliates also include some major developing-country NGOs such as Sri Lanka's Sarvodaya. While maintaining a special interest in assistance for refugees, ICVA's members to-day are engaged in a wide array of humanitarian and developmental activities. Much of ICVA's substantive work is carried out by its two working groups, on development issues and on refugees and migrations, and by sub-groups. A special fund facilitates the participation of developing-country agencies in ICVA activities. Financed by its member agencies, ICVA also receives outside contributions. In recent years, the principal external donors included the official aid agencies of Australia, Canada, Norway and Sweden, the Intergovernmental Committee for Migration, the Office of the UN High Commissioner for Refugees, the Ford Foundation and the World Bank (20). ICVA is also giving increasing attention to development management. In 1985 it launched its "Management for Development" programme with the aim of promoting and supporting appropriate management services for NGOs worldwide. The following year ICVA initiated an international seminar on "NGO Management Development and Training". As a result of this seminar, the NGO Management Network was established in February 1986 and subsequently three regional networks for East and Southern Africa, South-East Asia and South Asia. ICVA's management development programme receives support from Canadian CIDA and the Ford Foundation.

New perceptions in the 1970s

The 1970s were again marked by emergencies, such as in Bangladesh in 1971, drought in the Sahel region and Ethiopia in 1973-74, the end of the Vietnam war in 1975 with its sequel of massive refugee flows and the plight of populations in sealed-off Cambodia, Guatemala's earthquake in 1976, the flight of refugees to Somalia and to Sudan. Again, many developmental NGOs contributed to humanitarian relief in such situations, and some new NGOs were founded, in particular after the African drought.

A different organisational approach was adopted by some twenty NGOs from ten European countries and Canada. Following the African drought of 1973-74, they created a jointly funded agency to respond to some of the requirements. This was EURO ACTION ACORD, founded in 1976. It is active mainly in rural development in several African countries as well as income-generating activities for refugees and surrounding populations in various areas of Sudan. In 1986, with its name changed to ACORD and some changes in membership, and with a growing budget ($10.5 million), this consortium also evolved towards more decentralised programming -- to be done in Africa -- and the introduction of revolving funds to provide small loans in about half its programmes. A consortium approach was subsequently also mounted in 1979-81 by several European NGOs and one American NGO in a Cambodian emergency operation led by Oxfam. The late 1970s also saw a trend towards establishing permanent consultative umbrella NGOs in France, known as "collectifs d'ONG", and consortia of PVOs in the United States, such as PAID (Private Agencies in International Development).

Several factors marked a series of new perceptions and trends in the mainstream of NGOs' developmental work from the early years of the decade onwards. The experience gained by NGOs during the 1960s in the mobilisation against hunger and the myriad "micro" and other projects they had financed, and often directly implemented, led to some fundamental questioning of whether theirs was an appropriate answer. Over the years an awareness developed that mobilisation of good will was not sufficient, that poverty was the result of structural problems, and that some of the problems lay in economic relationships among countries, with so many of the poorer countries having to rely for their export earnings on primary commodities and fluctuating terms of trade. What could an NGO achieve, by its own resources, or even if its budget were multiplied a hundred times? Experience with field projects also led many NGOs to question the "technical assistance" nature of much of their overseas work. Development was perhaps not always a question of teaching a man to fish: much could be learned from local people themselves, and the initiative should be theirs. Further, many people had no access to water in which to fish: what answers could be sought for assetless people, the poorest of the poor? Some NGOs, especially in European countries and Canada, came to reflect on their action as part of a larger scene. A modest cut in the official aid budget could mean a much larger reduction in resources than the amounts which NGOs themselves could raise. The same was true of reductions in export earnings of developing countries compared with the resources made available by official aid: thus, development assistance came to be seen as part of a broader context.

Such questioning and experience with the dimensions of poverty led a number of NGOs to do research on these problems, and to evolve new forms of information and advocacy. Less related to fund-raising, these new activities sought to enlighten public opinion on structural constraints to development, and to promote support for developing countries' interests on occasions such as parliamentary approval of the official aid budget or in the framework of major international conferences such as the UN Conference on Trade and Development (UNCTAD). In 1976, in the wake of UNCTAD IV in Nairobi, a group of NGOs concerned that trade and development issues were insufficiently known and that their campaigning on these issues was too fragmentary, jointly established the International Coalition for Development Action (ICDA). ICDA maintains an active role in promoting public knowledge and awareness of such issues as trade and development, developing countries' indebtedness and many others through the publication of ICDA News, the organisation of meetings, contacts with DAC Members' delegations at international conferences, and contacts with the press.

This change in perceptions was shared by FAO's Freedom from Hunger Campaign when it added the denomination "Action for Development" to its name in 1970. The change implied stress on a dual task: first, stimulating a critical awareness of development issues, and, second, promoting the involvement of people in their own development by helping them analyse their situations and identify their problems, supporting their action without imposing ready-made solutions or models. The latter orientation, shared by many NGOs, considerably strengthened the notion of partnership, and led some NGOs to a critical revision of their technical assistance role. An extreme is represented by NGOs which limit their role overseas to a responsive role in funding. An example is the French Comité catholique contre la faim et pour le développement (CCFD), which as a rule does not supply personnel. It funds requests from trusted partner groups in the developing countries, and otherwise focuses on nurturing, informing and motivating its own home constituency, composed of hundreds of local groups all over France.

These trends continued to develop in the 1980s, with NGOs of the South emerging as actors alongside NGOs of the North, while the information activities broadly designated as "development education" and advocacy acquired new prominence on the agenda of the NGO community in DAC countries.

The extension of co-operation with the official aid agencies

The 1970s were also the decade during which the establishment of arrangements for official financial co-operation with NGOs was completed for DAC countries as a whole. A number of countries had already worked out arrangements of this kind (Germany and Sweden in 1962, Australia, the Netherlands and Norway in 1965, Canada in 1968). In the United States co-operation between the official and private non-profit sector goes back to the early 1950s. Other countries had previously had more limited arrangements for official contributions to selected categories of NGOs: France, for example, for the "oeuvres" (that is, social and developmental activities of missionary groups), and the United Kingdom for volunteer schemes. A lead was given in Europe by the Commission of the European Communities, which set up its cofinancing programme in 1975. Other countries followed soon. The United Kingdom, with its Joint Funding Scheme, in 1975, Belgium in 1976, and the French Ministry of Co-operation, with its first liaison unit with NGOs, in 1977.

New Zealand institutionalised financial co-operation with NGOs in 1974, Ireland in 1977. In 1975 the Canadian International Development Agency (CIDA) established an additional, smaller division for co-operation with international NGOs. This enabled it to support the institutional strengthening and the operations of a number of NGOs in developing countries by acting through international federations or partner groups in the industrialised countries rather than direct funding. In 1985/86, CIDA's International NGO Division disbursed C$ 15.9 million assisting about one hundred international associations and networks with grants ranging from C$ 7.2 million for the International Planned Parenthood Federation to C$ 250 for an association for the disabled in the Caribbean. To this day, this activity of CIDA remains a unique feature among DAC Members' official aid agencies.

Similar motives prompted the US Congress to create institutions providing direct support for local initiatives, the Inter-American Foundation (IAF) in 1971 and the African Development Foundation (ADF) in 1980. Up to 1986, IAF provided over 2 000 grants in support of the activities of some 1 700 NGOs in Latin America and the Caribbean, ranging from small groups of peasants involved in self-help activity at the community level to national-level organisations that provide support to many such initiatives. ADF only became operational in 1984. With a ceiling of $250 000 for individual grants, ADF responds to requests for grass-roots development and institution-building in Africa, relying upon African expertise.

Criteria and mechanisms for official aid agencies' co-operation with NGOs are considered in some detail later in this report (see Chapter IV).

The rationale given by governmental aid agencies for establishing financial support for NGOs are similar across the spectrum of DAC countries. Replies to a DAC questionnaire in 1984 on reasons for co-operating with NGOs showed that virtually all DAC Members saw co-operation as: 1) a way of making use of the special features of NGOs and 2) enhancing public interest in development issues in Member countries. Almost all Members also explicitly mentioned the strengthening of partner NGOs in developing countries as an important factor, and about half of them quoted it as a reason for co-operating with their own NGOs.

Among specific features of NGOs, the most frequently quoted by the aid agencies in their replies was their attempt to ensure that the poorest groups benefit directly from developmental activities. Other features quoted by governments include NGOs' capacity for innovation, their ability to mobilise popular groups effectively and to stimulate self-help activities, their capacity to adapt quickly, the personal commitment and dedication of their leaders, and their effectiveness in small-scale activities. Some of these features enable NGOs to act in sectors and with population groups which official aid reaches less well.

The impact which co-operation with governments has had on the NGOs themselves has not been sufficiently analysed -- for example, in terms of increases in scale of operations, professionalisation of staff, extent of familiarisation with the policies, practices and constraints of official development assistance -- for generalisations to be drawn with precision (21). Greater professionalism is frequently mentioned and increases over time in the average size of cofinanced projects can be documented. In some DAC countries, representatives of governmental and non-governmental organisations also indicate their concern that financial co-operation has taken some of the steam out of fund-raising and several reports express alarm at the risk of dependence. Nor can much be said on what internal consequences there may have been in the official aid agencies, except to mention that concern with poverty issues has led in some cases to closer consultation with NGOs, as in the case of the special unit "ES 31" in the German Federal Ministry of Economic Co-operation (see Chapter II) and some other cases.

Several considerations, however, may be put forward. The new importance attributed to NGOs by the official aid agencies in the late 1970s and early 1980s followed some disappointment they had experienced with the defective implementation of government-to-government projects, notably in such areas as rural development and health, and with discontinuation of activities once external aid was phased out. Increased concern with poverty in the 1970s and the questioning of the extent to which the poor were being helped by public-sector projects were also factors. Host-country systems and services were found by the aid agencies in many cases not to provide effective channels for programmes addressing, for instance, villagers and small farmers. Many of these factors are at the back of aid agencies' insistence, when considering NGO projects for cofinancing, on specifying how the activity is expected to be continued afterwards and host-country partner with which the NGO intends to work. Thus, the extension of cofinancing contributed to the heightened role of host-country NGO partners, which was to become a major issue by the mid-1980s.

Another result of co-operation is a change in how NGOs are seen, and what is expected of them as "development" agencies, in terms of the characteristics that distinguish them from official agencies. These questions are examined to some extent in evaluations of NGOs commissioned by official aid agencies (see Chapter V). Their role is often seen as complementary: for example, to alleviate some of the budgetary restrictions on governmental social services in parts of Sub-Saharan Africa. The debate on roles of NGOs within a broader development assistance framework continues. Qualifications to the notion of complementarity which have practical importance are that a number of NGOs do not share this notion and perceive their action as distinct or alternative, and that in official development agencies many of the staff involved in field operations are not active in seeking and identifying opportunities to co-operate with NGOs. Nevertheless, the concept of complementarity has gained ground in recent years and was enunciated in a resolution of NGO representatives at a DAC meeting in 1986 (see Annex 2). Acceptance of a complementary role of NGOs is reflected in instances of joint official/NGO activities in the field and in the growing practice of many official aid agencies to contract NGOs for the implementation of activities which are fully financed by an official agency in designated developing countries or specific sectors. Other factors may be involved in this practice. In particular, it may also help the aid agency to reduce its investment in qualified personnel or to lower its costs as compared with contracting consulting firms.

When NGOs are perceived as development agencies and potential partners of official agencies, a question arises concerning a critical size. Moving on from very small localised initiatives, larger NGOs have the capability of capitalising on a long experience in development work and evolve through successes and failures a know-how which makes them valuable partners for the official sector. A critical size is not the only requirement, but it is essential to some permanence of staff and to the development of an institutional memory, itself a prerequisite to retaining the know-how acquired with experience.

Another change brought about by co-operation, specificially with the Commission of the European Communities, is that some European NGOs also have access to substantial amounts of food aid, for emergency and other purposes. Some of these NGOs have linkages with CARE in the United States and Catholic Relief Services, others with the Caritas networks; other denominational and secular NGOs are also involved. Record Community levels were reached in 1986, with "standard food aid operations" of a value of 62 million ECU managed by 37 NGOs in 62 countries. The bulk of it was allocated for relief purposes in Algeria, Angola, Mozambique and Sudan with about 30 per cent for development projects; "emergency food aid" for a value of 72 million ECU managed by six NGOs in three African and six Asian countries; and 3 million ECU allocated in cash for food purchases by NGOs. (On the latter facility, see the Section on "Triangular operations" in Chapter III.) In addition, Community emergency aid programmes for a value of 15 million ECU were implemented by NGOs, mainly in Ethiopia, Sudan and to a lesser extent Uganda, including food and medical supplies. Food aid provided by the Community is additional to cash grants made available to NGOs through cofinancing arrangements for development projects.

A specially significant development related to financial co-operation with the Commission of the European Communities is the establishment since the late 1970s of institutional relationships between the Commission and NGOs of EEC member countries collectively. They involve representation of NGOs from twelve European countries in an annual general assembly in Brussels and in the election of a permanent EEC/NGO Liaison Committee (the liaison committee of development NGOs to the European Communities) and its working groups. Together with ICVA, this institutional set-up in the EEC is the most significant international consultative and liaison network of NGOs from DAC countries. The two bodies cover different geographic areas and international linkages remain weaker between NGOs from North American and Pacific countries and those in Europe, particularly from Latin cultures.

The much greater focus of NGOs in the 1980s on economic, income-generating activities may also be traced in part to the experience acquired in projects cofinanced by the official sector. Other factors have played a role as well, including the deepening involvement of many NGOs with partner groups in developing countries, many stemming from or working with extremely poor people. Also, many NGOs are concerned about the viability of projects which they carried out in social sectors, and recognise the need for an economic base to sustain them. But this is a particularly difficult area of activity -- a difficulty compounded by NGOs' policy of working in the most deprived areas and with the most deprived population groups -- and a number of evaluations show that the record of NGOs is more uneven in income generation than in providing social services. The shock of the African famine in 1984-85 further strengthened the focus on "economic" projects, as well as the perception that complementarity between the official and private sectors is in the best interest of intended beneficiaries. There are efforts to articulate such complementarities more clearly (see Conclusions).

NGOs' co-operation with official aid agencies also has a political dimension. NGO activities aimed at giving poor people more of a say in their societies by definition means change. This can have a bearing on existing power structures, whether at the local level or in broader contexts. One should be aware that in a number of developing-country contexts NGOs may therefore be perceived as a threat. There have been many occasions on which official agencies, in negotiations and dialogue with host-country governments, have acted in support of NGOs, helping to win recognition of their autonomy and their roles. Official agencies often insist on having access to local NGOs in order to support their programmes in such areas as education and training. On the latter point, UNICEF in particular appears to have a record worthy of notice.

The 1980s: a view from within DAC countries

Some of the main features of the contemporary NGO scene form the object of more detailed consideration in subsequent chapters of this report. Certain points, however, deserve mention in a view "from within" DAC countries. These mainly concern NGOs' fund-raising activities, the constituencies which support them and changing orientations in NGOs' messages in reaching public opinion. Challenges were raised at mid-decade by the African famine. Once more, new initiatives were launched by people of goodwill, as witnessed by many examples such as Band Aid or the Austrian foundation "People for People" ("Menschen für Menschen", set up in 1983 and active in relief and subsequent agricultural projects particularly in Ethiopia), to quote just two. The repeating of disasters is leading to the evolving concept of the right on the part of victims of emergency situations to humanitarian assistance and the duty on the part of states to contribute to such assistance. [See the resolution of the First International Conference on Humanitarian Law and Ethics organised in Paris in January 1987 by Médecins du monde and the Faculty of Law of the University of Paris-Sud, with the participation of the President of the Republic and the Prime Minister of France, in Le devoir d'ingérence by Mario Bettati and Bernard Kouchner (Denoël, Paris, 1987).] Lessons from the emergency and from responses, in particular those of young people through Band Aid, deserve further consideration. These points are outlined in the next sections of this chapter.

Fund-raising activities and national constituencies

For DAC countries taken together, only about one third of NGOs' expenditures represent contributions from the official aid agencies (this proportion varies considerably from country to country, as shown by Table IV-1 in Chapter IV). NGOs' own resources have various origins, depending on the country.

Tax arrangements are important sources of income in some countries. In Germany, in particular, the so-called "church tax" (designating the redistribution to churches of a fraction of income taxes of citizens who are members of churches) is a major source for churches, thus for the developmental programmes which they finance. In a number of DAC countries, fiscal incentives have been established for private and corporate gifts to charities (including developmental ones) in the form of deductions from taxable income. In the United Kingdom, in addition, a tax recovery scheme entitles registered charities actually to receive from the tax system an additional 43 per cent of amounts donated in the form of "covenants", whereby individuals pledge fixed monthly contributions for amounts and charities of their choice over a period of at least four years. Since April 1987, special tax relief is also granted to individuals for gifts up to £100 deducted by employers from payrolls -- another form of donation which minimises administrative costs for NGOs. According to a recent survey of tax incentives, Japan and the United States are top of the charts (22).

For a great number of NGOs fund-raising is the major source of income. The churches mainly rely on collections, and the main collection specifically devoted to aiding developing countries takes place at Lent. The basic sources of income for NGOs are appeals through press advertising, posters and the mail; legacies; regular contributions and membership fees; corporate gifts (the latter, of far greater importance in North America than in Europe). Most governments attach importance to NGOs' capacity to raise funds from the public at large or from specific sections of the national community. This is implicit in their having established "matching grants". It is partly a way to increase resources. At least as important for some governments, however, is the commitment of home constituencies, and the measure of people's trust for beneficiary NGOs which donations represent.

For NGOs themselves, raising their own resources is a guarantee of independence and autonomy vis-à-vis the official sector. On the other hand, NGOs have no assurance that their efforts will give the expected results. These efforts must be continued year after year or throughout the year to raise the resources needed.

Co-operation with governments has made it more common for NGOs in some DAC countries to indicate their sources of income: these, and their expenditures under various categories, are published yearly for PVOs registered with AID in the United States. (In 1985, registered US PVOs received donations in cash for $991 million, in supplies and equipment for $174 million, and in services for $23 million.) In several DAC countries, however, not all NGOs publicise this information, although they provide it to the official service in charge of regularly collecting the data, for DAC statistics among other purposes. DAC statistics only collect data on NGO grants on a national, not an agency, or sector or geographic basis. Undoubtedly, published data on fund-raising developmental NGOs would be desirable in DAC countries where it is still not customary.

In France, in 1985, the structure of NGO resources was as follows:

	FF million	Per cent
1. Private, total	<u>938</u>	<u>71.1</u>
of which:		
Gifts and legacies	647	49.0
Membership fees	52	3.9
Grants from other French private agencies	15	1.1
Grants from foreign private agencies	33	2.5
Other	191	14.5
2. Official, total	<u>382</u>	<u>28.9</u>
GRAND TOTAL	1 320	100.0

Source: Commission Coopération Développement, Argent Associations Tiers monde, Enquête d'estimation de l'aide privée française au développement mise en oeuvre par le canal des associations de la loi de 1901. La documentation française -- Ministère de la coopération, Paris, 1988.

Fund-raising operations may be, and sometimes are, entrusted to professionals. In many cases, however, they are the result of efforts of committed individuals and groups, in parishes and other communities. Substantial backing from constituencies gives some NGOs a measure of continuity. Constituents' groups are also active in organising meetings, lectures, discussions, shows, etc. The churches are an obvious example. Approximately 2 000 informal groups all over France back the "Comité catholique contre la faim et pour le développement". (The active constituency of CCFD in 1982 included 4 500 regular contributors, 85 committees established within dioceses and 1 900 local teams with an estimated 18 000 people who contributed time and energy to organise 3 200 meetings.) Based on 1984 figures, a recent study estimates that the number of Canadians directly participating in the work of NGOs may be as high as 40 000 of which the vast majority -- perhaps 90 per cent of the total -- offer their time on a voluntary basis. These in-country volunteers are mainly assigned to fundraising and administrative/clerical tasks (Bridges of Hope? op. cit.).

The active home constituency of Oxfam in 1982 included 3 000 "collectors", 20 000 women and men working unpaid in Oxfam shops, and 650 Oxfam groups linking some 300 000 donors. By 1986, Oxfam's 800 shops had become the agency's major single source of funds (£14 million in a total of £45 million in the financial year ending April 1986), with cash donations in the form of response to appeals, covenants, legacies, etc., amounting to over £13 million. Oxfam has a policy of restricting the share of public-sector funding in its annual budget to less than 10 per cent, to maintain autonomy.

Mani Tese is believed to have the highest share of private donations in its budget of all developmental NGOs in Italy. It counts on some 1 600 members, 30 000 sympathisers and 46 groups in various parts of Italy (23). Mani Tese was established informally in 1964 within a missionary framework in response to the concern of groups of young people with world hunger issues. It became an association in 1966. Its honorary president is the Frenchman Abbé Pierre, founder in the 1950s of the "Emmaus" permanent communities offering shelter, food and work to marginalised poor people in France.

Most NGOs necessarily have to invest some of their resources in fund-raising activities. Expenditures for this purpose amounted to $79.7 million in 1985 for US PVOs registered with AID, accounting for 3.4 per cent of their total expenditures (including official funding) or 5.4 per cent of the resources they raised privately (24). Similar shares were reported in 1985 for French NGOs: FF 53 million, accounting for 4.2 per cent of total expenditures or 5.7 per cent of privately raised resources (25). But a number of NGOs in fact devote a higher share of their total expenditures to fund-raising and publicity: 12 per cent for Médecins sans frontières, 15 per cent for Oxfam in 1982, 18 per cent for Foster Parents Plan in the United States in 1985.

It has been suggested that fund-raising in some western countries, whether done by churches or secular NGOs, ultimately addresses much the same Christian public, and that in countries such as France, which have seen a decline in numbers of practising Christians, this source might dwindle over time. Another concern is the ageing structure of active supporters of certain NGOs. The good response of young people to the Band Aid/Live Aid appeal for Africa in 1985 may not imply (some believe) that younger generations would be ready to undertake as well a protracted activist rôle in supporting developmental causes and agencies.

Certainly, the critical dependence of many NGOs on success in fund-raising has implications for their capacity to plan. An element of "volatility" is inherent in people's response to appeals. Rigorous attention to management problems, irreproachable accountability, and professional quality in the conduct of publicity campaigns and related research and techniques can limit the risks of such volatility. Failure in a single costly publicity operation may entail dismissal of paid staff and reductions in planned overseas activities: examples exist.

For many smaller NGOs, the most serious need is to build up a more secure financial base in order to continue and develop their work. Retaining capable permanent "core" staff working full-time is a must to this end (the same applies to NGOs in developing countries), inevitably entailing administrative costs. In many cases NGOs' administrative costs are reported to be significantly lower than those of official aid administrations: 3.5 per cent of total expenditures for Oxfam in 1982, 6 per cent on average for PVOs registered with AID in 1985. Experienced operators estimate that administrative and fund-raising costs average about 10 per cent of expenditures of well managed NGOs. Accountability to constituencies dictates that they should be kept as low as feasible. Resources for administrative costs are supplemented by cofinancing projects with official aid agencies, by charging a fee (7.5 per cent in the Netherlands, for example, but the share can be higher in other Member countries).

A point which has come to the fore quite recently concerns the way in which NGOs evolve over time. From small beginnings, highly motivated and willing to confront difficult situations, there is a danger that NGOs may reach a stage of conservatism, complacency and bureaucratisation. Substantial resources from the official sector may encourage such a trend. It seems indeed that in certain cases NGOs do not age well, and that relatively secure resources and perhaps also growth in size beyond a certain threshold endangers such essential features as the willingness to innovate, and to stay close to the poor. If these dangers are real, what remedies are there? How can large and financially secure NGOs avoid turning into something similar to parastatal organisations, losing touch with their constituencies and with the original purpose for which they were set up? There are not many longitudinal studies of individual NGOs to throw light on these queries and on the internal management and monitoring systems which might help to guard against the dangers of an ageing process. Oxfam believes that its decentralised organisation through field directors seeking local initiatives to support has helped it maintain flexibility and capacity for innovation. A recent Canadian study suggests that the main point is to maintain a self-questioning attitude and that this is much helped by agencies' involvement in field work (Bridges of Hope? op. cit.).

Changing orientations in NGO messages to public opinion

Another difficult -- indeed controversial -- aspect of NGOs' publicity for fund-raising relates to the messages and images conveyed. There is a dilemma here between, on the one hand, attaining results in terms of donations and, on the other, coherence with other aims of NGOs of building up an interest among the public for longer-term developmental issues, beyond the emotional response to emergencies, and hence conveying images which respect the dignity of developing countries' populations and emphasize their own efforts.

There has been much heated debate on these issues, with NGOs accused of promoting "hunger pornography" to enhance fund-raising. A first comment is that NGOs' appeals are often made for raising resources in response to emergencies: unfortunately, starving children and other images of desperate deprivation are not things of the past. There have been instances when governments stepped in with relief on a scale commensurate with needs only following the surge of emotions raised by NGOs and the media in the public at large. The most recent example relates to the African emergency of 1984-85 when pictures of the Ethiopian famine started to be shown on television in late October 1984.

A second point, however, is that rousing people to give is more easily done by striking the chord of emotional response. To enhance fund-raising, NGOs have frequently publicised images only suited to emergencies, thus constantly conveying a perception of human beings in developing countries as intrinsically passive recipients of aid which is ultimately degrading. Publicity of this kind has also encouraged an identification of NGOs with relief, and led to frequent underestimation of their development role.

In the early 1980s a few NGOs started revising the messages carried by their appeals for non-emergency aid, and made them more coherent with the evidence from experience and the orientations of their broader development education activities (e.g., appeals explicitly conveying the message that feeding a child is only part of an answer: the child's mother should also be helped, and educated to feed it better; a publicity campaign built around the slogan "give them the water and they will grow their own food"). Over the past two to three years, the movement towards a revision of NGOs' publicity from this standpoint has gathered strength.

A workshop organised by the UN Non-Governmental Liaison Service together with ICDA and ICVA in Geneva in November 1985, on the theme "NGOs and Africa: A Strategy Workshop", was an important step in this process. [See in particular John Clark (Oxfam), "Presentation on Fund-Raising and Development Education", and the report from Working Group 2, "Development Education and Campaigns", in NGOs and Africa: A Strategy Workshop, 14-17 November 1985, Final Report, UN-NGLS, Geneva, NGLS/86/3, 1986.] A "priority message" from the workshop was that positive images of people and development possibilities in the South, including African NGO roles, should be conveyed in development education and publicity. Participants also committed themselves to evolving a code of ethics in NGO fund-raising consistent with development education objectives. These were to stress interdependence. A target of 10 per cent of individual NGO resources was recommended for development education. The concept of a "code of conduct" in fund-raising is gaining acceptance.

Lessons from Band Aid/Live Aid

Some points related to the Band Aid/Live Aid phenomenon -- the most important fund-raising event ever, in response to the largest emergency of this decade so far -- will conclude this general discussion of trends. Led by Bob Geldof, a man who had no particular doctrine to propose, "except concern, no message except the individual's responsibility to care", the Band Aid response to famine in Africa raised $110 million in a few months.

In fund raising, it evoked an enthusiastic response from young people, potentially unlocking a new constituency for developmental NGOs. Which of its features made for success? Several have been identified: the involvement of the media; the feeling of hope in Bob Geldof's message; the communion across national frontiers in a basic human purpose; Bob Geldof's age and style and the spontaneous and instant nature of the whole phenomenon.

Although there were criticisms -- mainly because the simple or simplistic hunger/gift reflex was reinforced -- in the opinion of analysts from the NGO community Band Aid/Live Aid offers positive challenges. The events which prompted the campaign were a harrowing reminder of the failure of national, international and voluntary agencies' policies in relation to agriculture and food provision. The active participation of young people in Band Aid's success may in part have stemmed precisely from the fact that it did not arise from the ranks of professional development agencies. Whether or not the generous compassion of Band Aid can be sustained in the future and translated into support for concerted policy action depends, to some extent, on how the established voluntary agencies respond to the challenge. Development and justice work has become increasingly difficult in the economic and political climate of the late 1980s. Just as NGO strategies for tackling development issues need to change, so do the methodologies of their campaigning and education work. Band Aid demonstrated the need to start at the beginning with people's perceptions of the issues and not with the NGOs' "well worked out, predetermined causes and solutions". Changes would imply engaging the public in discussion, stimulating more interaction between NGOs and the public, concentrating less on lectures and papers by experts, recognising the potential of popular culture and gearing more programmes towards young people. [Colm Reagan, "Live Aid: A Challenge to the 'Experts'?", in Trocaire Development Review 1986, Dublin 1986. See also John Clark, op. cit.]

Band Aid also deserves mention for its subsequent management of funds, through reputed accountants' firms, and their utilisation, with a highly professional and committed voluntary advisory group in charge of project selection to allocate the 60 per cent share set aside for long-term development activities. Band Aid chose not to become "operational" itself (with the single exception of transportation of emergency aid) but rather to channel funds to projects submitted by existing agencies. The appropriation of funds for long-term development has taken much longer than originally expected (between March 1985 and October 1986, $71 million was disbursed of which $44 million for immediate relief). Delay in identifying good longer-term projects is not surprising, especially considering that Band Aid's mandate for funding long-term activities was limited to six African countries, all of them "least developed" and three of them at war or affected by civil war (Burkina Faso, Chad, Ethiopia, Mali, Niger and Sudan). Band Aid set strict criteria for its contributions for solving longer-term problems: projects should reduce vulnerability to famine in the long term; proposals should contain evidence that they have been informed by local initiative and demand; projects addressing the hundreds of thousands of orphan children without resorting to institutionalisation would have been warmly welcomed but failed to materialise. The process of selection continued in 1987 and the winding up of the administrative unit in London in charge of the transfer of funds to approved projects was expected to take place round the end of the year, after publicising total expenditures. Reports on expenditures so far show that assistance has flown through over 120 different agencies. The feeling of urgency associated with Bob Geldof's message in 1985 contrasts with these delays, but the difficulty experienced in identifying good projects for funding in a short time is not restricted to Band Aid nor to the NGO sector.

NOTES AND REFERENCES

1.   Ernst Michanek, Role of Swedish Non-Governmental Organizations in International Development Co-operation, SIDA, Stockholm, 1977. Extracts are published in The Role of Non-Governmental Organisations in Development Co-operation, Liaison Bulletin Between Development Research and Training Institutes, New Series, No 10, Development Centre, OECD, 1983.

2.   US Non-profit Organisation in Development Assistance Abroad, TAICH Directory, 1983.

3.   American Association of Fund Raising Counsel, Inc., Giving USA: 1982 Annual Report, quoted by H.R. Roberts, "The Domestic Environment of AID-Registered PVOs: Characteristics and Impacts", in Robert F. Gorman (ed.), Private Voluntary Organisations as Agents of Development, Westview Press, Boulder, Colorado, 1984.

4.   The Economist, July 25, 1987 and Internal Audit in Charities, The Institute of Internal Auditors, London, 1987.

5.   Directory of Non-Governmental Organisations in OECD Member Countries Active in Development Co-operation, 2 vols., OECD, Paris, 1981.

6.   Le Tiers monde que faire? Répertoire d'adresses utiles 1987, Ministère de la coopération, Paris, 1987.

7.   Directory of Non-Governmental Organisations in Japan Concerned with Development Co-operation, Ministry of Foreign Affairs, Tokyo, 1985. A more fully informative Directory was published in 1988, providing data on the activities, income and expenditure of 174 NGOs who replied to the questionnaire (out of 275 agencies contacted): Japanese NGO Centre for International Co-operation, Directory of Non-Governmental Organisations in Japan -- NGOs active in Development Co-operation, March 1988.

8.   Canadian Council for International Co-operation, ID Profile, A Who's Who and What's What of International Development, Ottawa 1986.

9.   Voluntary Foreign Aid Programmes 1982-1983, Bureau for Food for Peace and Voluntary Assistance, AID, Washington, 1983.

10.   Cf. "Dossier" on development NGOs in The Courier, No. 104, July-August 1987, CEC, Brussels.

11. Brian Smith, "US and Canadian PVOs as Transnational Development Institutions", in Gorman (ed.), op. cit. There is a difference in scale and related appreciations between the United States and Europe: two of the three agencies quoted by Brian Smith had resources of the order of $20 million per annum in 1985.

12. Arthur Kilgore and Curtis Roosevelt, "The Non-Governmental Organisations and the United Nations", in Douglas Williams, The Specialized Agencies and the United Nations. The System in Crisis, C. Hurst and Co., London, in association with the David Davies Memorial Institute of International Studies, London, 1987.

13. A fascinating account of the missionary and various denominational origins of a number of US NGOs is provided in John Sommer, Beyond Charity: US Voluntary Aid for a Changing World, Overseas Development Council, Washington, DC, 1977. Extracts are contained, under the title "A History of Good Deeds: for Better and for Worse", in The Role of Non-Governmental Organisations in Development Co-operation, Development Centre of OECD, op. cit.

14. Ben Whitaker, A Bridge of People. A Personal View of Oxfam's First Forty Years, Heinemann, London, 1983; and Rodolfo Casadei, "Oxfam: A Success Story", in Dimensioni dello sviluppo, 1987, No 2, pp. 6-28, Associazione Volontari Servizio Internazionale: AVSI, Cesena, Italy.

15. Voluntary Foreign Aid Programmes, 1985, Bureau for Food for Peace and Voluntary Assistance, Agency for International Development, Washington, DC, 1986.

16. On US PVOs' relations with the government, seen through the history of the American Council of Voluntary Agencies for Foreign Service -- which in 1984 merged with a consortium of PVOs, Private Agencies in International Development, to establish the new umbrella organisation INTERACTION -- see Elizabeth Clark Reiss, ACVAFS: Four Monographs, The American Council of Voluntary Agencies for Foreign Service, New York, 1985. This publication also offers insights on issues which still figure prominently in NGO debates today such as the autonomy of NGO, the risk of dependence on the official sector, etc.

17. See for example Gabriel Marc, "Les organisations privées d'aide au développement en France", in Etudes, Paris, November 1982.

18. G. Marc, op. cit., estimated that about one third of the resources of the French Catholic NGO "CCFD" were devoted to non-ecclesiastical partners by the early 1980s.

19. Bernard Kouchner, Charité Business, Pré aux Clercs, Paris, 1986.

20. See ICVA's brochure Twenty-Five Years and Beyond, Geneva, 1987.

21. See, however, the paper by Charles Elliott, "Some Aspects of Relations between North and South in the NGO Sector", in the Special Issue of Autumn 1987 of World Development, (No. 15, Supplement, edited by Anne Gordon Drabek), Pergamon Press, on the March 1987 Symposium on "Development Alternatives: The Challenge for NGOs", organised in

London by the <u>World Development</u> journal and the Overseas Development Institute. This paper suggests that modernisation goals may have received more emphasis than empowerment (in the sense of helping beneficiaries to acquire sufficient experience and capability to decide for themselves what can be done to improve the condition of their lives, and to carry through the action required) as a consequence of official sector funding. See also <u>Bridges of Hope?</u>, op. cit., in particular on the impact on NGOs' programmes of official aid's contributions for predetermined countries or sectoral activities (summarised under Chapter V of this report).

22. <u>A Comparative Study of the Tax Treatment of Donors to Charity in 35 Countries</u>, Interphil House, Yalding, Kent, 1987.

23. Giuseppe Scidà, <u>L'utopia concreta. Indagine sulla Associazione Mani Tese</u>, ed. Franco Angeli, Milan, 1987.

24. <u>Voluntary Foreign Aid Programmes, 1985</u>, op. cit.

25. <u>Argent Associations Tiers monde</u>, op. cit.

Chapter II

SUPPORT FOR NGOs OF DEVELOPING COUNTRIES
WITH REFERENCE TO AFRICAN EXPERIENCE

The term "NGOs of the South" is widely used to designate a great variety of associations and local organisations of developing countries. Some of these are affiliates of international NGOs with national branches both in developed and developing countries. In a number of cases, affiliates in DAC countries have supported initiatives of sister organisations in the developing world. An early example is the Young Christian Women's Association: as early as 1946-49, an experienced woman professional from the YWCA in the United States helped the YWCA of India to establish the first School of Social Work in that country. In more recent years, a similar spirit led the Commonwealth Professional Association, a loosely knit umbrella body for 31 Commonwealth professional associations (architects, engineers, land surveyors, nurses, etc.), to initiate various activities: e.g., a training conference for selected magistrates from six African countries to improve their capacity as in-service trainers; or a fund for the purchase of journals and visual aids by member societies with foreign exchange restrictions.

In the vast range of "NGOs of the South" certain development-oriented organisations which became visible to "the North" in the mid-1980s appear to hold potential for enabling the poor to improve the circumstances of their livelihood and over the longer term to have more of a say in the directions of development in their societies at large. They therefore deserve special attention. These mainly include:

-- Self-help groups at local grass-roots level;

-- Their unions at higher levels up to national federations; these associations of local groups may perform functions such as lobbying in capitals as well as rendering services, e.g. in training, credit, accounting, to their affiliates;

-- NGOs which promote and support local groups through the provision of training, technical advice, credit, the establishment of networks, etc. ("support institutions" or "service NGOs"), but are not membership organisations themselves.

Some NGOs of DAC countries are now working with these particular categories of institutions, some others have been supporting them for decades. Official aid is also increasingly involved, whether directly or by support through Member-country NGOs. In Germany, for example, working with a non-profit local organisation in the developing country, is a criterion of the Ministry of Economic Co-operation in allocating funds to German NGOs. This chapter attempts first to delineate local organisations, their various stages and the forms of support which have best suited their development. Then it provides relevant illustrations drawn from African experience. Relevant recent research on experience in other parts of the world, particularly Asia, is highlighted in the following chapter.

1. LOCAL "SELF-HELP" ORGANISATIONS

In recent years, as they acquired experience in working with grass-roots organisations, NGOs and interested researchers increasingly perceived local organisations as intermediaries in development. Their role was found to be critical in strategies of rural development aimed at both improving productivity and distributing its benefits more equitably among the rural majority. Potentially, the most dynamic local institutions were found to be locally based membership organisations -- co-operatives, farmers' associations, mothers' clubs, health committees, water users' groups, tenant leagues and the like, which Esman and Uphoff designate as local organisations (1). They are also widely known as "self-help" organisations.

They are defined as organisations which act on behalf of, and are accountable to, their membership, and are involved in development activities. There has been research on their role in overcoming poverty, and much firm evidence has already been drawn from experience. Selections are offered from authoritative reports, which are listed in the notes and references at the end of this chapter.

In the United States, the study of local organisations by Esman and Uphoff, based on an analysis of the literature and of 150 relevant cases, concludes that "while other components (infrastructure investments, etc.) are necessary, no strategy of rural development combining growth in productivity with broad distribution of benefits can be visualised in which participatory local organisations are not prominent". In Europe, action-research conducted since 1983 by a special unit in the German Federal Ministry for Economic Co-operation (BMZ) has reached positive conclusions on the potential of local self-help organisations for overcoming poverty. In 1983-84 the special unit "ES 31" of the BMZ, previously known as "S 24", investigated 25 self-help initiatives and promotional institutions, particularly in the credit sector. It then surveyed other instruments and organisational approaches for the promotion of self-help, studying eight more cases. The findings of this special unit, operating in liaison with other official and voluntary agencies, have been reflected in German official policy statements on the role of self-help organisations in aid and poverty alleviation.

The main conclusions of S 24/ES 31 studies up to 1986 were that the cases studied amply demonstrated that the poor are able to organise themselves and to save, meaning that they can increase their income and pay for part of the services received from supporting institutions. Indigenous promotional and supporting institutions have an important role in helping the processes by which groups get organised and then facilitating their access to the services of the formal sector. Once this has been achieved, formal-sector institutions can also contribute to a broad-based process of economic and social development which involves the rural poor. Aid from industrial countries can also play an important supportive role in this process by facilitating and encouraging co-operation between local self-help groups and promotional indigenous institutions (mainly non-governmental) as well as with formal-sector institutions (mainly owned or controlled by the government).

"ES 31" is currently engaged, together with 18 governmental and non-governmental German and foreign agencies, in stimulating and assisting innovative schemes in support of self-help, especially in the financial sector. An example is an Indian-German five-year pilot project aimed at improving access to credit by the poor, led by the Indian National Bank for Agriculture and Rural Development (NABARD) and Germany's financial aid agency (KfW), with the participation of Misereor and several Indian institutions. This pilot project, started in December 1985, builds on relevant experience of official and non-governmental agencies in facilitating credit for the poor in India. The activities of "ES 31" to promote self-help are followed with special interest by the official aid agencies of the Netherlands and Switzerland (2).

Why self-help?

"What course [asks Bernard Lecomte referring to drought-prone regions in Africa] is open to villagers in the Savanna, where rainfall is sparse and erratic, other than to pool their energies to modify the slopes and control the watercourses? Surely collective effort, for them as many others, must necessarily precede individual advancement. (3)" Examples from quite different circumstances: women street vendors in Indian cities, landless people in rural Bangladesh, small farmers in Thailand, likewise demonstrate the benefits brought to the group or community, and to the individuals themselves, by poor people who pooled their energy and mobilised their resources to improve their lives.

Functions of self-help organisations in rural development

Functions of local organisations relate to efficiency, equity and empowerment (4). To take but one, efficiency, Esman and Uphoff find that in resource-poor environments, where governments lack the funds, personnel and administrative capacity to provide relevant services, self-help groups can play an important role by:

-- Providing more accurate and representative information;
-- Adapting programmes to priority needs;
-- Providing opportunities for group communication;
-- Mobilising resources on a self-help or matching grant basis;
-- Providing locally appropriate technical knowledge;
-- Enhancing utilisation and maintenance of facilities and services;
-- Enhancing co-operation in new programmes involving economic, social or technical change.

Origins of self-help groups

Self-help groups start in a variety of ways. They are initiated by:

-- Villagers without previously recognised leaders -- as in the village of Wuro-Sogi in Senegal;

-- Local leaders or innovators -- as with the "Naam movement" in Burkina Faso, revived by a Burkina Faso sociologist;

-- Shared initiatives between locals and outsiders -- as in the encounter of an Italian retired teacher and an Indian innovator at the origin of the Sarva Seva Farms/ASSEFA association in India; or the NGO "Six S" in Sahel countries;

-- Government agencies -- e.g., the Malawi self-help water supply committees; and

-- Foreign NGOs -- including religious groups, private voluntary organisations like Oxfam, and others such as universities, research institutes and foundations.

In Africa, the centralised and directive stance taken over the past two decades in rural development by many governments, often with external assistance, has not provided productivity and distributive benefits. It has led to activities focused for a long time on individual ("pilot") farmers, to enforced co-operativism or service-intensive and often narrowly sectoral programmes. It has diverted attention from farmers' and villagers' groups and their own needs, aspirations and potential contributions. A recent Dutch evaluation of rural development activities in Burkina Faso and Mali (see Chapter V) gives an idea of the uphill road now faced in the more deprived areas of those countries. René Dumont, the French agricultural development specialist, highlights the economic rationale for extension of small irrigated plots managed by farmers' groups for food self-sufficiency and environmental protection in the "Fleuve" region of Senegal and neighbouring regions in Mali and Mauritania. He contrasts this with the mediocre results of capital-intensive and directive public corporations which continue to operate there (5). Similar views are held by an official donor, Switzerland, which has paid attention to the strategic implications of backing local small-farmers' associations as from the emergency phase of its aid in poorer areas of the Sahel after the famine of 1984-85. In reviewing Swiss emergency aid to drought-affected areas of Burkina Faso, Mali and Niger, an evaluation report notes the similarity of activities undertaken by local groups with this aid in the three countries: environmental protection and improvement works centred on water preservation and implemented with "food for work", "counterseason" production of food crops particularly vegetables, and the construction and stocking of cereals banks by groups of villages. It notes the dismal failure of large-scale projects and the somewhat greater inclination of governments to focus more on smaller local projects with no recurrent-cost implications and involving local population groups in a responsible way. Finally, it recommends continuing Swiss aid over several years for small projects aimed at food self-sufficiency and drought prevention, at the initiative of local communities (6).

Notwithstanding constraints, in West and Central Africa private non-profit regional training institutions with a strong focus on rural promotional work, such as CESAO and INADES (both originally founded by religious orders), played a considerable role over almost three decades in laying the ground for the subsequent development of self-help groups. These

41

institutions, created in the early 1960s, were supported with a good measure of continuity over the years by several official and non-governmental sources. In 1970-75 the first village groups started emerging in Burkina Faso, Mali and Senegal. Contacts among group leaders were favoured by their training institutions. In 1975-80 the first associations of groups were formed. In many parts of Burkina Faso and Senegal, villagers' groups and unions spread because one or more villagers -- men or women -- had received suitable informal training at CESAO and were motivated in working towards improving life in their community.

Stages in the development of self-help groups

It would be risky to generalise about the sequence of stages in the development of self-help groups. There are differences between countries and between types of experience. With this caveat, sequences in the development of farmers' groups in West Africa and particularly Burkina Faso and Senegal over the past fifteen years can be sketched as follows (7). The "innovator", man or woman, who is almost invariably found at the origin of grass-roots organisations, can only achieve something if he identifies and motivates other people in the community. Qualities needed are those of a social innovator, not just a rebel. Initial scepticism in the community gives way to hope only when the first results emerge. This stage -- when the leader is seeking his way and at the same time trying to win over companions -- is the most difficult. Many initiatives disappear after one or two years, because of resistance or opposition. The innovator can escape rejection only by negotiating skilfully, demonstrating what the scheme holds for each and every one, and disarming opposition.

In the subsequent process of group forming, the focus moves from the leader to the nascent grass-roots organisation: by far the best is to leave people to devise and implement simple schemes without suggesting particular approaches or deadlines. This corresponds in large measure to what observers in other parts of the developing world have called a "learning process" approach to development. This approach rejects blueprints. It recognises that rural people need the opportunity to adjust the activities and management of their local organisations to what they learn from experience (8).

The key to a group's organisation is the mobilisation of its own resources: creativity, by thinking together and among equals, and contributing fees, savings and work. It is important that a first venture should have a good chance of succeeding and involve all concerned, each according to their ability. Contributions mean cash and a cash-box, and that conjures up many trials and tribulations. Administering the funds together, with arrangements to avoid temptations, builds up mutual confidence. Decisions are then taken by members of the group, if possible with all the villagers, on what is to be done and how it is to be achieved. At this stage, the community chooses who will run the operation, who will record and appraise the results, and what resources will be used.

When a group has succeeded in its first operation, chosen its leaders and started to fill its cash-box, it is time for it to find out what others are doing elsewhere, to travel and visit other groups, discuss difficulties, hear what other people besides the innovator/founder have to say. Seminars and workshops can also be useful if outside participants do not come to sell particular prescriptions but share doubts and problems, help the group clarify its thinking, and bring out what has been left unsaid.

A group is bound to come up against problems that it has not encountered before. It may make mistakes. Much good can come from failure if initiative and self-criticism are given full scope. Self-appraisal is an essential tool: stopping to look back at what has been done, analysing what failed and what succeeded, deciding how to go about the next tasks.

These initial stages may typically take two to five years. But an African rural leader has said that it took him seven years to get the group properly established in his village. He then travelled to other villages in the area. It took him another year to convince the authorities that he was not a trouble-maker, and three more to bring together groups from his own and neighbouring villages in an association, without heading it himself.

From a local group to an association of groups

Village-based development cannot be put on a sound footing without the gradual establishment of a network of rural communities initiated by the local organisations themselves. Various frameworks exist to help this process along. A regional training centre, for example, can help people to become acquainted, arrange tours and meetings, and so on. This process takes time and resources. An example of an association of groups is the Committee for Development Action in the 16 villages of the Bamba-Thialène area in eastern Senegal (department of Tambacounda), which developed from 1976, comprising villagers from the three ethnic groups of the area. From the beginning, this association devoted a share of the sale of communal fields' produce to provide part of the funding needed for core personnel and administrative costs (9). Over-rapid growth makes an association unwieldy: feuding and malpractice emerge, mistrust reappears, the incentive to reach out is lost.

Leadership training is recognised as a major task of associations of self-help groups with respect to their affiliates. Another challenge is how to ensure that associations effectively represent their member groups and are controlled by them. Training in accounting and management at all levels may be critical to this end.

Esman and Uphoff (op. cit.) did research on the impact of vertical and horizontal linkages, and of participatory and egalitarian orientations on the performance of local organisations. On vertical linkage, they found that regionally or nationally federated local organisations tend to be found in the more successful categories. But their success require good understanding by "outside" supporters of the linkages involved. Among structural features, horizontal linkage is one of the factors most closely related with performance. A participatory orientation is important even when the structure of local society is against it: indeed, within an adverse local environment, local organisations have less success than the average unless they are highly participatory and egalitarian in their operations. Governments and other organisations seeking to promote local development in adverse local conditions need to be aware of this constraint.

2. STRATEGIES FOR EXTERNAL SUPPORT: ILLUSTRATIONS FROM WEST AFRICA

Strategies for external support should be long-term, combining efforts and resources of several foreign NGOs and, where appropriate, official aid. Rather than directly subsidise individual local groups, they should identify promising support institutions, not excluding host-country governmental administrations when these have services for rural institutions. Direct aid to individual local groups can be provided in response to requests of the groups concerned through funds available for small-scale activities, within, for instance, the discretionary limits of embassies, but such case-by-case interventions do not by themselves add up to a strategy. Small grants for local initiatives may represent a first step, however, in areas where populations have not recovered from an emergency and institutional growth poles are weak or non-existent: an official aid agency is currently doing this by organising food-for-work projects and distributing small grants for local initiatives in just such an area in Mali. But other types of support must become available to sustain the process of group forming.

A first point is that aid should be appropriate to the various stages of group organisation and proportionate to the group's own efforts and capacity: a schematisation is drawn in the next section on the basis of experience in West Africa where these self-help movements have gone farther than in other parts of the continent. The sequence as depicted requires the existence of support institutions: to provide training, for instance, based on suitable experience and methods.

Adapting aid to stages in group organisation

Experience from French-speaking West Africa is in line with experience elsewhere in suggesting that project aid from donor agencies, including NGOs, is overgenerous with technical assistance and temporary resources and introduces inappropriate blueprints. Furthermore, timing in the release of project funds often does not coincide with the seasonal timing suitable, for agricultural or labour-availability reasons, for carrying out the proposed activities. Until local groups are strong enough to make the project part of their own strategy, project aid tends to weaken rather than strengthen them. A strong group is one that has developed a negotiating capacity, a financing capacity with resources of its own so as to be a real partner in a joint venture, a design capacity, and a capacity for implementation and management so as to maintain control even if part of the operation is let out to contractors.

At stage 1, which is often loosely defined as a "pre-project" phase, little direct financial aid should be supplied (experienced practitioners doubt that project aid may be appropriate before stage 3 is reached; hence the cautiousness in defining the initial stage as a "pre-project" one). Groups should be encouraged to establish and expand community savings-and-loan schemes. The most useful aid will be virtually invisible, exploring what the group needs to do in order to operate more effectively and more reliably: extending its membership, acquiring training and experience in management, associating with other groups, giving women the courage to meet among themselves, promoting literacy, or checking abuse. Support may also be needed to help the innovator and founder to devote time to the group; and to survive. In initially less promising areas, "action research" programmes may help develop or revive some form of local association. Two to five years may be required for this stage. Paradoxically, it is this first stage with its modest direct funding requirements which is less likely to find the appropriate kind of support, unless the interested donor is willing to act through the building or strengthening of support institutions. Unfortunately, it is often at this very tentative initial stage of grass-roots organisations that aid inputs are supplied in the form of grants for micro-projects. These may help provide a somewhat better response to a felt need but they are rarely given in adequately repeated and durable fashion to represent more than a drop in the ocean. Rather than help people get organised, they may lead to a temporary grouping for the only purpose of implementing the micro-project. Finally, this aid for precise purposes may be excessive relative to people's own efforts and may indeed discourage mobilisation.

At stage 2, the grass-roots organisation has become active at village level and within a small area of several villages, and has demonstrated a capacity to run its own activities. Financial assistance is now timely and needed, so that the organisation can in its turn support the activities of its members. Two conditions have proved essential: first, funds should not be earmarked in advance, since it is the members of the group who must decide which of the many pressing and necessary actions should be supported (not all the schemes will prosper, but at this stage resources will be spread among a host of small schemes, thereby reducing risks); and, second, part at least of the aid should be repayable, not directly to the funding agency but to locally managed funds for new activities in the community or in its neighbourhood. Grant aid is also needed however for training and part of the physical investment and operating costs. To avoid the customary growth of operating costs, a ceiling can be set on foreign assistance available for this purpose (e.g., 12 per cent), or aid can be gradually phased out over several years (eight for example). Supporting institutions have an essential role to play at this stage in helping the group constitute resources of its own, for example by aligning the aid input with the volume of self-help (subscriptions, repayments, value of days of labour), and by careful management of funds financed by loan repayments, e.g., through capitalisation. Stage 2 may last between six and ten years.

At stage 3, the group should be in a position to contact other sources of external funding, but also come gradually to rely on traditional sources of finance: their own community savings schemes and banks. There is not enough experience at the time of writing to detail this third stage further, except for a few examples: some local associations in Burkina Faso, for instance, were beginning to receive decreasing amounts of funding, nine years after the start of operations of the funding intermediary NGO "Six S". Literature on local organisations in other parts of the world does not offer many indications on activities which reach or approach a self-supporting stage. One of the few known examples is the comprehensive rural health project of Jamkhed in India. This exemplary experience, started in 1971 by an Indian medical two-person (husband and wife) team, now covers 175 villages and 200 000 people with health care and production-oriented services, self-help village institutions and continued in-service training, in the drought-prone and poor area of Jamkhed in the state of Maharashtra (10). In general, the problem of adequate resources for the "core funding" of support institutions beyond the duration of aid is far from solved.

Support institutions

The functions and time needed for promoting and strengthening local organisations clearly go beyond what an official aid agency, and many NGOs, can undertake directly. The funding agencies which have been interested in such promotion so far generally act in partnership with "intermediary" supporting institutions, several of which may be involved in a given area simultaneously. This is borne out by African experience, by successes and also by failures in cases where intermediary institutions were not established and grass-roots organisations not consistently supported. African experience with support institutions and strategies for the promotion of local self-help organisations is more limited so far in duration and country coverage than is the case in Asia. As already mentioned, this is due largely to the highly directive and centralised stance of government in rural development over the past two or three decades in many African countries. In several instances, therefore, NGOs involved in rural development in Africa have co-operated directly with governmental services. ACORD, for instance, has only recently started to operate directy with nascent village associations. Another reason for failure to find local support institutions in Africa is that donor NGOs in many cases did not understand existing traditional associations which were out of keeping with their own models. The NGOs were more interested in operating "their" project in a given locality than in developing a long-term supportive strategy and building up intermediary institutions. Major exceptions are found in some French-speaking West African countries and Zimbabwe and, to a lesser degree, Kenya (where local initiatives, especially women's, abound, but general strategies and supporting institutions do not). The remainder of this chapter is concentrated on a few interlocking features of experience in West Africa. Many of these features, such as the key roles of mobilisation of people's own efforts and of credit, match the more general lessons drawn from research on successful developments in other continents.

3. ILLUSTRATIONS OF SELF-HELP MOVEMENTS FROM AFRICAN EXPERIENCE

The experience described in the following sections brings out the role which two particular categories of support institutions are currently playing in several Sahel countries:

-- Associations of local farmers' and women's groups;

-- Intermediary institutions which provide technical support and obtain suitable funding from European NGOs for financial support, partly in form of grants, partly in loans for revolving funds, for these associations of local groups.

As mentioned previously, this whole movement, which has by now reached a significant scale, in particular in Burkina Faso and Senegal, was initially promoted by yet another type of support institution: regional training centres providing informal training to ordinary villagers.

At local level: the village of Wuro-Sogi

Situated at a crossroad in the north-eastern river region of Senegal, in the department of Matam, Wuro-Sogi has a population of 10 000. About one-fourth of its labour force migrated years ago to Dakar and France: migrants started funding a "caisse d'entraide" (mutual help fund) in the 1960s. Following the drought of 1973, the hardship experienced by villagers with inadequate water supplies led them to pool their efforts and savings over five years to purchase a motor pump, whose maintenance and fuel consumption (50 litres of fuel per day) they continue to fund. By 1985, 244 homes were connected to the water system, financed by families' contributions to the communal water fund. Wuro-Sogi migrants and local villagers established a three-branched development association. The Dakar branch is specially in charge of relations with government services. The Paris branch looks after fund-raising and extending contacts with interested French people, mainly farmers. Through voluntary monthly contributions, other small projects have been carried out: a mosque, a square where discussions can be held, schoolrooms, storage for cereals, etc. Women took responsibility for some of the tasks of common interest: waste disposal, a communal vegetable garden. Negotiations with interested foreign NGOs took time before one NGO agreed to support the village's own projects: a millet mill for women, the village pharmacy. Now, a French NGO is helping establish an initial communal field of 30 hectares, on which to experiment with dry season irrigation techniques and grow more food. Additional seedlings are grown for people from other villages in the area to take away. Adults alternate in communal work so as to spread improved practices to individual plots. Village assemblies made plans in 1987 for literacy courses and improvements to the school. Decisions are taken by consensus, after exhaustive discussion, gradually overcoming traditional discrimination by age, sex and caste (11). Through its development association, this village is linked vertically with the federation of farmers' associations of Senegal (FONGS) and with Senegal's consultative NGO forum CONGAD.

An association of groups: the Naam movement

"Développer sans abîmer" (development without damage) is the motto of the Naam movement, revived by a Burkina Faso sociologist since the 1960s among the Mossi people in the Yatenga region of Burkina Faso. Traditionally, naam was a temporary sharing of tasks by young people for activities of common interest, such as the organisation of feasts. The revived movement aims at accumulating surplus to invest in developmental activities. Defined as a "pre-co-operative movement" by its founder, it is based on subtle perceptions of changing traditional and modern values.

The movement speaks to young people and women in the first place, gradually drawing in the village as a whole. Activities during the rainy season mainly concern communal fields, with such cultivations as millet, cotton, sesame and peanuts. In the dry season, when traditionally agricultural work came to a stop and youths and adults had to migrate to earn their keep, three kinds of activities are undertaken.

-- Community activities for environmental protection and improvement: ditches and small dams, wells, land-shaping to halt erosion, communal forestry, fuel-efficient ovens and improved pots, etc. These activities are subsidised, labour is paid daily wages.

-- Income-generating activities: vegetable gardening, animal husbandry, handicrafts, millet mills. Inputs such as tools, equipment, animals (poultry, rabbits, sheep) are financed on loans. Proceeds from sales are shared in varying proportions between amortization and the provision of capital for new projects.

-- Social and cultural activities: theatre, sports, dancing, functional literacy, training, village pharmacies, etc. These are subsidised.

The Union of Federations of Naam Groups grew from approximately 100 groups (men's, women's or mixed) in 1973 to over 2 500 in 1987 (12).

A national federation: FONGS in Senegal

La Fédération des ONG du Sénégal (FONGS) is a national federation of small farmers' associations. It originated from a meeting of leaders of farmers' groups in Dakar in 1978, obtaining legal recognition four years later. The first few years were not dynamic: many affiliated groups were inexperienced or had problems, funds and time were lacking for initiatives at the federal level. Difficulties were gradually overcome. With support from early partners -- the French ACCIR (Association champenoise de coopération inter-régionale) and the Dutch NGO NOVIB -- the federation became significant as from 1985. Small, medium and large associations of farmers' groups are affiliated to FONGS, numbering in 1987 200 000 members and an estimated one million people including families.

FONGS is not a financial intermediary. Its role is basically advocacy, promotion and diagnosis. It sees training and credit as twin pillars for building a better rural society in the country. A specialised service is in charge of training, mainly in accounting and management, and a unit is in charge of promoting savings and credit activities. Ultimately, the aim of FONGS is to meet the challenge of hunger through strategies for food self-sufficiency. It currently receives support from an array of foreign and international NGOs, including the African Development Foundation, Brot für die Welt, the Dutch NGO CEBEMO, the Ford Foundation's Dakar office, Oxfam and "Six S". From 1987-88, a special training programme for women, with women as trainers, will start responding to the needs identified in consultation with women all over the country: in management, agricultural techniques, cooking and food preservation.

With support from the International Development Research Centre (IDRC, Ottawa) FONGS convened a seminar in Dakar in June 1987 to seek solutions for the new credit problem faced by small farmers in Senegal. The former system of subsidised credit for agricultural inputs and equipment had been abolished, leaving both a vacuum and bad habits among farmers as concerns loan reimbursements. Credit could be obtained only from donor NGOs, but this was limited to the particular localities where they operate, or from the national institute for agricultural credit [Caisse nationale de crédit agricole sénégalaise (CNCAS)], with ceilings on lending as a result of current measures for national financial reconstruction. Further, CNCAS' lending was highly selective, favouring ventures with assured returns (whereas there is no certainty in rainfed agriculture in Senegal), and it required a down payment of 35 per cent of the loan, and guarantees on the remaining 65 per cent.

Interest rates were above 10 per cent, which experience suggests is a maximum for agriculture in Senegal. Finally, CNCAS staff were unfamiliar with small farmers' requirements and the workings of their associations. Faced with these problems, FONGS is proposing a series of activities aimed at raising incomes and savings. These activities include the creation and management of stocks of seeds, fertilizers and village cereals banks, with expanded communal fields to help create food reserves between harvests, using food aid for setting up revolving funds, increasing crop diversification and off-farm rural job creation, and appropriate training including literacy. The aim over the next three years is the establishment of a savings and loans systems, with written transactions and accounting, within each small-farmers' group. Special efforts are envisaged to involve women in these activities. The intention is to create a national system of savings and credit unions over a ten-year horizon. FONGS looks to external donors, both official and private non-profit, to help it establish funds which may enable CNCAS to extend credit lines to small farmers' associations. It also asks them to assist the activities outlined above. Given the need for inputs and credit, measures of this kind are certainly needed to prevent a decline of small-farmers' production and income (13).

In other parts of Africa, there exists a number of local groups, and associations of groups, but rarely up to the level of national federations. Among major associations in other African countries one may quote the Organisation of Rural Associations for Progress (ORAP) in Zimbabwe, founded in 1980. By 1984, ORAP linked over 300 local groups (14).

The support strategy of "Six S"

Founded in 1976 as a "common tool" for associations of groups in several countries of West Africa, "Six S" (Se servir de la saison sèche en savanne et au Sahel), an international NGO based in Geneva, is a financial intermediary and support institution. Its denomination reflects the potential of the dry season, when agricultural activities traditionally came to an end, for implementing environmental improvement works of common interest, mostly based on water conservation and the use of water for out-of-season production of food crops. Remunerating labour for these works can reduce seasonal migration and over the longer term can provide opportunities for a sounder village economy and improved life-styles.

"Six S" is currently active in Burkina Faso in liaison with the Union of Federations of Naam Groups, in Senegal in liaison with FONGS, and, to a lesser extent so far, in Mali and Mauritania. Its strategy embodies the principles outlined above, departing from the project approach and suiting aid to the various stages of group organisation. In addition to channelling funds to local programmes, "Six S" devotes a sizeable share of its resources to training activities. Its founders include Africans and Europeans involved from the start in various capacities in the development of self-help movements in French-speaking West Africa.

From its inception in 1976, "Six S" negotiated with potential donors the establishment of a flexible (non-earmarked) grant fund, to be available on the spot as a credit line with disbursements to be effected on the basis of locally designed programmes and requests formulated by designated local area ("zone") committees. A part of these funds was to be disbursed in the form of loans, thus initiating revolving funds for new activities. Several donor agencies -- the Swiss government and four European NGOs, notably Misereor and CEBEMO -- met the challenge and contributed to a renewable flexible fund which was extended as trust built up on the basis of experience and evaluations.

The local structure developed by associations supported by "Six S" is based on "zones" (in Burkina Faso, these correspond to the arrondissement or district level). A zone comprises several groups active in the same small area which elect a zone committee.

The distribution of funds among zones in each country is decided, on the basis of the number and activities of associations in each zone, by the Board of "Six S", which meets in Africa once a year. Each zone is aware at the beginning of the dry season (October) of the amount of foreign aid which will be available to it by the beginning of the dry season the following year. "Six S" does not intervene in the distribution among village-level groups: each local group negotiates amounts with its zone committee. Funds are extended in the form of loans (generally for a duration of five years and at slightly below market rates) for productive projects and as grants for larger physical infrastructure of common interest and for workers' training schemes (chantiers écoles), which provide much of the labour for infrastructure.

Accounting is a core activity of groups and is also centrally monitored by the supporting institution itself. At village level, accounting of "Six S" funds is kept by a young literate villager. The cash-box is entrusted to an elder, or the fund is transferred to a bank account requiring three signatories together (president, treasurer and a group member). Within the village, the management of activities such as the cereals bank and the millet mill come under the responsibility of committees often including women, thus increasing opportunities for managerial experience. In addition, at zone level, accounting is also kept by the more fully trained zone delegate, designated by each zone and salaried by "Six S". Loan reimbursements in local currencies are placed in separate accounts directly owned by each zone and managed exclusively by delegates of the groups in that zone, to enhance self-financing capacity and independence vis-à-vis "Six S".

Control is likewise three-tiered: at village level, by group members, with supervision from the zone delegate; at zone level, by the zone committee and an accountant from headquarters; at headquarters by the board, which includes delegates from zones and groups and controls the executive secretary. A professional auditing firm in Switzerland audits, advises and at times provides specialised training.

In addition to ensuring funding through its own channel, "Six S" convenes ad hoc consultations between potential donors and individual associations for additional activities (15).

4. DIVERSIFICATION OF SUPPORT: THE FUNDING CHAIN

As shown by the examples given so far, self-help groups and support institutions are often aided by many sources. In the first place, many NGOs derive a part of their resources for operations in the field from their country's official aid agency, and in many European countries the EEC, thus involving donor countries' public sector as a third partner in their relationship with local organisations. Over the years, many local groups find opportunities to enlarge their range of donors, large and small. Encouraging an NGO of the South to diversify its sources of support is recognised as an indication of successful institution-building on the part of the initial partner.

The "project chain", however, challenges traditional financial reporting requirements. Recognising the plurality of sources, donors which support rural grass-roots movements in West Africa acknowledge in many cases that financial reporting should no longer be kept separately for each donor according to its own reporting requirements. It has to be replaced by periodic auditing by independent professional auditors providing a full and accurate picture of income and expenditures from all sources. This greatly simplifies the task for the recipient and also gives donors a guarantee of the recipient's accountability. This shows that flexibility in funding NGOs is compatible with accountability while flexibly supplied aid can have a cascade effect through reimbursements to locally managed funds.

5. NETWORKS

The importance of exchanging experience directly among agents of change engaged in similar activities but in different contexts is widely recognised. Such exchange is a feature of group organisation. Asia in particular has a rich and varied experience in local self-help organisations in both rural and urban settings, relevant to similar movements in other developing regions. In Africa itself, as in Latin America, countless initiatives stand to gain by finding out how a similar problem was solved by other groups. There exists a great number of networks to perform these functions.

For self-help organisations, the role of networks may be illustrated by IRED (Innovations et réseaux pour le développement), an international non-profit association, mainly oriented towards South-South exchange. Founded in 1981 with initial support among others from Canadian CIDA, IRED is not a financial intermediary or funding organisation, but a "facilitator", a promotor of associations, which also provides technical support for training, management, organisation and appropriate technologies. Based on a small secretariat in Geneva, and with regional representatives in several developing countries, IRED's board comprises eight representatives of self-help movements and independent research institutes from Africa, Latin America and Asia, and one for Europe and North America. Membership in the IRED association is on a personal basis (170 members from approximately 50 countries), while partner associations (mainly from the rural sector and informal urban sector), and research institutes, numbered approximately 800 in 1987.

IRED provides support for local associations and networks, based on a continuously up-dated identification of new partners. In 1985-86, three IRED seminars enabled self-help associations to set up national or inter-country networks in Central, Southern and West Africa. It organises exchanges, specialised seminars and meetings, e.g., among leaders of grass-roots organisations, farmers of different continents, women responsible for women's vocational training in different countries. Its quarterly bulletin, IRED-Forum, published in English, French and Spanish (4 000 copies and 15 000 readers, 85 per cent of which in developing countries) contributes to the exchange among groups and networks.

As illustrated by this example, networks are another point of entry for foreign aid wishing to provide appropriate support for the development of grass-roots movements. But the funding of networks is part of a strategic approach which is not yet so widespread as needs and opportunities demand. Indeed funds are relatively readily available for "projects", but not so for the "core funding" of institutions without which the projects cannot be formulated. Indeed, virtually all costs are overheads in organisations whose functions are promotional and supportive, as is the case of networks among others. Their activities are "invisible" compared to construction or land reclamation. In addition, "invisibility" also applies in the sense that core support cannot easily be attributed to any specific donor source.

6. NGO CONSULTATIVE GROUPS AND POTENTIAL FOR IN-COUNTRY CO-OPERATION

Over the past few years, NGOs of the North and the South have set up consultative fora within developing countries. In Africa, these have been established in Burkina Faso, Mali, Senegal, among others. The scope of in-country consultative fora where NGOs (both external and domestic) meet may be somewhat limited by the heterogeneity of their constituencies. Such fora, however, have a role in reciprocal acquaintance and exchange of information. Participants at the DAC seminar held in June 1986 also thought these consultative groups could perform a useful role in designating NGO representatives for attendance at in-country co-ordination exercises, such as UNDP round tables, where a full representation of NGOs operating in the country would be unwieldy. In addition, in-country NGO fora have proved themselves in some instances operationally relevant during emergencies, as was the case in Mali in 1984-85. Consultative fora would benefit by having specialised services attached to them. For example, in Burkina Faso two European NGOs have established small services to assist their own partners with technical aid for project preparation and management. Services of this kind may be particularly useful for NGOs operating in the same sector of activity.

At the initiative of the consultative group of NGOs in Senegal, the Conseil des ONG d'appui au développment (CONGAD), a network was established in June 1987 among African NGOs [Forum of African Voluntary Development Organisations (FAVDO)]. The idea was first discussed by African NGO leaders at the UN General Assembly's Special Session on Africa in May 1986.

Funded by the Norwegian aid agency NORAD, a survey was recently conducted for the International Labour Organisation (ILO) on the potential for co-operation with NGOs in rural skills development. It covered Kenya (where some 400 NGOs are at work, mainly in the most deprived areas), Somalia, Tanzania and Zambia. [M.J. Culshaw, Consultant, Opportunities to Promote Rural Skills Training for Productive Activities through Enhanced Co-operation with Non-Governmental Organisations, ILO, document 8417f, February 1987.] The study may be of interest beyond ILO itself. Its main conclusion is that a wide variety of practical activities could usefully be developed to improve the quality of rural skills training for youth and the effectiveness of income-generating activities for women. In order to do this, an active "search of NGOs" should be undertaken, followed by provision of technical support to NGOs for such activities, which in the case of ILO could be done through a regional presence. The report provides up-to-date information on arrangements for in-country NGO co-operation in the four countries reviewed. Prospects for collaborating with government services are generally positive. NGOs' resources are frequently overstretched, given their proximity to communities in desperate socio-economic situations. There exist in those countries thousands of groups of women who need to improve their social and economic position. Tragically, they lack needed support and very few groups are successful. The report suggests proposals for initial action to develop in-country co-operation to improve income-raising and training activities for local groups.

7. SOME CONSIDERATIONS FROM REAL-LIFE EXPERIENCE

Some considerations from the viewpoint of local communities described above will conclude this chapter. One relates to reciprocity within a North-South context at the grass-roots level. The village of Wuro-Sogi in Senegal was given an unusual opportunity when the director of a juvenile offenders' service in the city of Valence, France, had 24 young people sent there for a few weeks to help villagers make bricks for the cereals bank. Each youth was hosted by a family whose life he shared. After this experience 21 of them could be taken off probation and resumed a normal life in France. Villagers were pleased and felt this was the first time they had been able to share something with foreigners.

As a result of close co-operation within developing countries with local organisations, donor NGOs may come to appreciate their partners' experience and insights and wish to share them more broadly with their own staff. An example is provided by a major Italian NGOs' federation, FOCSIV, which since 1984 has invited African experts to contribute to the training imparted to its volunteers before their departure overseas and organises sessions in Africa for the training officers of its own Italian affiliates at African institutions such as INADES, CESAO, the Pan-African Development Institute (IPD). Participants at the London meeting in March 1987 reminded Northerners that immigrants from developing countries offer opportunities on the spot for improved human relationships. The French CCFD organises visits of representatives of its partners to France to meet constituents' groups, and more recently started promoting reciprocal visits by French groups. Elements of reciprocity form part of the research led by the NGO Terra Nuova of Rome for the conference on the "image of Africa" mentioned in Chapter VI. African researchers were for once involved and the views of African groups were sought on their self-perception and their image as conveyed in Europe.

Visits can also be organised in undiscerning fashion: a well-known piece in the literature on "development tourism" provides a good reminder (16). A recent example was provided by 40 separate study tours of farmers from a European country in one dry season to visit a local union of farmers' groups in Senegal, just then undergoing a difficult period of reappraisal. In that particular case, the hospitality costs involved made it necessary for the union to charge a small daily fee per visitor, something the organisers had forgotten to plan for.

The experience of Wuro-Sogi also offers a viewpoint on instances of poor fit between the grass-roots level and some larger projects. At the time of writing, the village was working, as mentioned above, with assistance from a foreign NGO at mastering the techniques of irrigation on a communal field of 30 hectares, planned to reach 100 hectares within a few years. Indeed, village elders worry together with active members of the association -- the latter are, typically, men of 35 or 40, who were children at the time of independence -- about future prospects for young people, now that recruitment in the administration or migration are no longer an option. They realise the basis of their livelihood has been destroyed by the drought -- and want to rebuild it, with such modifications as are needed: irrigation in the dry season, planting of fruit trees in the communal field now that wild species are dead, nurturing of trees for firewood, etc. (Villagers, who are Moslems, decided that the water they use for ritual cleanliness five times a day, would not be wasted: it is used to water the young trees of the village wood plot.) Young people, especially those who went to school, lost the traditional know-how and had to learn farming from scratch. Up to a few years ago, many villagers did not send their children to school. Now they feel that it is "their" school: they want all the children to attend, but they also discuss how to modify the curriculum to include know-how that is relevant to daily life, e.g. by taking care of a school garden.

Yet, the latest village assemblies were worried. Two nearby dams were nearing completion (17). What impact would they have on their lives? Would their land be taken away from them and re-assigned by the state-owned corporation in charge of the irrigation schemes? Nobody seemed to know.

Villagers of Wuro-Sogi also think of expanding their pharmacy, where drugs are obtained for a fee so as to restock when needed. Medicinal plants will be grown on the communal field. Migrant workers send discarded medicaments which they obtain from friends in France. Nearby, a 300-bed district hospital, built by foreign aid and staffed for some years by foreign technical co-operation, now lies unstaffed. How many village pharmacies in the country could have been started and maintained with the money invested in that hospital? Will the hospital, to which patients came even from nearby Mauritania, become operational again? Again, nobody knows.

Together with the credit problems now faced by small farmers in Senegal and evoked in the section on FONGS, these examples from the experience of a village underpin the need for a better match between user-populations' resources and public-sector planning, investment and services especially when, as is the case in Senegal and many other low-income countries at present, public-sector resources are severely constrained.

NOTES AND REFERENCES

1. Milton J. Esman and Norman T. Uphoff, Local Organisations -- Intermediaries in Rural Development, Cornell University Press, 1984.

2. Federal Ministry for Economic Co-operation, Final Report of the Special Unit "Fighting Rural Poverty through Self-Help" (ES 31) on the second Working Phase (October 1984-April 1986), ES 31, E 8000-35/86, 2 vols., Bonn, April 30, 1986.

3. Bernard Lecomte, Project Aid, Limitations and Alternatives, Development Centre Studies, OECD, 1986.

4. Esman and Uphoff, op. cit. On the word "empowerment" see footnote 21 to Chapter I.

5. René Dumont, Pour l'Afrique, j'accuse. Le journal d'un agronome au Sahel en voie de destruction, Plon, Paris, 1986.

6. B. Younoussi, D. Ouedraogo, Rapport d'évaluation du programme Nothilfe Sahel au Burkina Faso, au Mali et au Niger, DDA, t.311 Sahel 8, Berne, January-March 1986.

7. This and the following three sections are largely based on Lecomte, op. cit.

8. See also David Korten, "Community Organisation and Rural Development: A Learning Process Approach", in Public Administration Review 40, No. 5, 1980.

9. A case study of Bamba-Thialène is presented in Sharing Experiences in Development, report of a workshop for development leaders, Harare, Zimbabwe, June 1984, Silveira House, P.O. Box 545, Harare, or IRED, 3 rue Varembé, CH 1211, Geneva.

10. Margaret Wolfson, Community Action for Family Planning: A Comparison of Six Project Experiences, Development Centre Studies, OECD, 1987.

11. Thierno Aliou BA, "Pratiques éducatives, mutations sociales et dynamisme villageois dans la moyenne vallée du Sénégal. La fonction éducative des associations de développement dans les communautés villageoises. L'exemple de Wuro-Sogi, 1969-1987", doctorate thesis, Department of Education, University of Lyon II, April 1987, 285 pp., unpublished.

12. Bernard Ledea Ouedraogo, "Les groupements Naam" in Culture et développement, FOCSIV, Milan, 1987.

13. FONGS, B.P. 269, Thiès, Senegal.

14. Cf. Sharing Experience in Development, op. cit.

15. Fernand Vincent, Etude de cas "Six S" -- Stratégies paysannes, document, IRED, Geneva, May 1984; J.-M. Pradelle and H. Jorritsma, Quand les villages du Sahel s'organisent, report to the Club du Sahel, 1987. The Club du Sahel is preparing, for publication in 1988, a comprehensive report including the above and drawing as well on similar studies of small-farmers' associations in Mali and Senegal.

16. George P. Butler, "A Plea for Visitor Ethics", in OECD Development Centre, The Role of NGOs etc., op. cit. and Robert Chambers' analysis/critique of "rural development tourism" in Rural Development: Putting the Last First, Longman, London, 1983.

17. On these dams (Diama and Manantali) and related irrigation schemes, see René Dumont, op. cit.

Chapter III

SELECTED ISSUES AND ILLUSTRATIONS

Local self-help organisations hold the most promising potential on the NGO scene to-day for overcoming poverty. This explains the interest of several official aid agencies, donor NGOs and researchers. Experience and research in this field have led to clarification of the concept of replicability, a concept which is particularly associated with NGOs, and to viewing it increasingly as a question of institution-building, linkage to government services, empowerment and what Prof. Uphoff calls "extendability" to underline that "replication" in this sense cannot be achieved by turning on a xerox machine and reproducing identical copies across the landscape.

Their contribution to institution-building is therefore increasingly seen as one of the key criteria in assessing NGO performance. There exist indicators to judge to which extent the indigenous organisations supported by donor NGOs have become autonomous institutions. Experience acquired by Asian organisations promoting self-help among the very poor in Bangladesh and India provides insights on the impact of organisations. These have been recently researched by the Ford Foundation, seeking common traits of organisations with greater impact. Experience of this Foundation in community-based management of irrigation and forestry resources in South-East Asia suggests that more mature ("third generation") NGOs could play a larger role in micro-policy reforms, through processes by which services in areas at sub-national level could more cost-effectively match the needs and resources of local populations. A donor NGO in the Netherlands is now extending beyond credit institutions the scope of action-research on self-help initiated by a special unit in Germany (referred to Chapter II). The purpose is to clarify how best donor NGOs can support strategies for the promotion of self-help. An important tool for strengthening local groups and organisations is "self-evaluation", especially when used regularly over time as part of management. A first part of this chapter draws on recent research on these important features of local self-help organisations. Support for self-help groups necessarily implies involvement in economic activities, as income generation is a central feature of such groups. The remaining sections of this chapter consider some aspects of NGOs' raised interest in supporting "economic" rather than social projects: in particular appropriate technology and indications from experience with the promotion of small enterprise. Finally, some information is provided on "triangular operations" in food supply in Africa and on new forms of assistance which are being developed by some NGOs such as funds for extending credit guarantees and investment funds to support small enterprise in developing countries.

1. INSTITUTION-BUILDING

"Replicability" has often been perceived in an almost mechanical way. It is only recently, and mainly through evaluations, that inquiry into the potential for replicability has shifted to factors such as the adequacy of local leadership training or a deliberate search for contact with governmental services and other potential partners, in order to adapt and replicate a particular "model". At a DAC preparatory meeting in November 1985, which planned for the seminar held in June 1986, participants from both official aid agencies and NGOs questioned the concept of replicability and suggested alternatives which from their experience appeared to be more pertinent. Is replicability a question of multiplying the number of projects or increasing the scale of individual projects from small to large? Participants agreed that sustainability or viability rather than replicability should be the main concern. External NGOs can have a stimulative and supportive role, especially in the key area of training, but progress comes from local groups and societies. The real issue is how to develop the dynamics of self-reliant continuation: how local groups can master their own development and make their voice better heard through South-South exchanges and participatory evaluation. It is a question of assisting developments with a probability of survival, with institutions whose roots will grow. Related to this, is the fact that many NGOs engaged in development activities face organisational and management problems. For this reason management development has become a priority for a large number of NGOs and NGO networks. Recently several management programmes have been developed, including consultancy activities, training seminars and the production of management manuals. One example is the Canadian support through two non-profit organisations: the Manitoba Institute of Management (MIM) and the Montreal-based Gestion Nord-Sud, which are active with both NGOs of the South (Africa, Indonesia and shortly the Caribbean) and with NGOs in Canada.

Rationale for institution-building

Several donor agencies, both private and official, are increasingly concerned with the strengthening of local self-help organisations. They are looking at the economic and political need to achieve higher returns from the large investments made in educational and service delivery institutions (with related recurrent costs), and in infrastructure for agriculture and rural development. Such expenditure is likely to yield low returns unless intended beneficiaries are brought together in counterpart organisations, enabling them to benefit from public policies and services, contribute to service costs, participate in service management and promote their common interests. Furthermore, governments that face severe limitations on funds and trained manpower cannot manage rural development without the participation of rural people of all classes, an argument which has been gaining in importance in recent years. Investment is thus equally needed in institutional and human resource development. The role of NGOs in assisting such developments is currently one of the main points in relevant research.

A major study of NGOs in rural development, the 1985 report by Bertrand Schneider to the Club of Rome [Bertrand Schneider, The Barefoot Revolution. A Report to the Club of Rome, Intermediate Technology Publications, London, 1988] based on an in-depth survey of 93 projects in

Africa, Asia and Latin America, reached the conclusion that NGOs play a unique and largely successful role in assisting and strengthening local groups and associations, most of them with a productive component. As "enablers", NGOs raise the consciousness of villagers, including women, helping them to organise self-help groups and undertaking training in health, family planning, environmental protection, etc., motivating participants and up-grading their skills.

Yet it appears that for many NGOs institution-building in developing countries is not currently a priority objective.

Spectrum of external NGOs with respect to institution-building

A study by Brian Smith at MIT of NGOs from Canada and the United States, currently under way and expected to be completed by the end of 1987, sketches three categories of NGOs (1). One includes disaster relief agencies, diversified at subsequent stages with developmental activities. The second consists of technical assistance providers. A third category groups institution and network builders.

The attitudes of the first two groups have not changed significantly over the years. Only the third group has come to view development as an essentially indigeneous process. A few church development agencies and secular NGOs have maintained a consistent record of support for locally organised initiatives. While they are occasionally involved in community support, the approach of the first two categories remains one in which they themselves define the local problem and solutions (e.g., food aid, small-business assistance) and then involve a counterpart institution in programme implementation. Many NGOs still operate their own programmes, maintaining much of the control as well as their positions as providers for the poor, and identifying projects and needs in sectors and areas in which they have expertise.

This characterisation of North American NGOs applies to voluntary agencies of other DAC countries as well and deserves elaboration. In the first place, it may be observed that the approaches to developmental work of the first two categories imply disbelief in people's own potential for progress, contrary to findings from experience. Evaluations of what happened to a project five or ten years after the phasing-out of external aid are rare, and few are made public. Findings provide sobering indications of disappointing longer-term results of acting as providers and implementers, with no further involvement beyond project duration. Lack of maintenance by non-involved beneficiaries, resulting in constant new project requests for the same initial purpose, is amply documented for irrigation and water supply schemes.

Several factors may thwart a more consistent search for institution-building by NGOs: e.g., the long-term nature of this kind of work; a lack of inclination to discuss one's proposals with poor communities in far-away countries; the weight of tradition and gearing of procedures towards precise "projects"; reluctance to commit resources for goals which cannot be fully specified at the outset; and, possibly, the temptation to expand the portfolio of operations of a more classical type with the benefit of official contributions. Maintaining control is another likely reason: few voluntary agencies so far have accepted the calculated risks undertaken by CEBEMO, Misereor and others in supplying the type of credit-line funding which is not earmarked. Another serious constraint is the unwillingness of many external NGOs to contribute to the operating costs of their partners in developing countries. This attitude is still widespread, as exemplified by charitable/developmental bodies which still perceive as wasteful the funding of salaries for local delegates or representatives of local groups for performing organisational tasks. This reflects an unwillingness to nurture local groups which are independent of the charitable or developmental NGO itself.

As mentioned previously, however, the goal of strengthening institutions and local partner groups in developing countries is increasingly seen by DAC official donors as one of the main factors in their rationale for cofinancing with NGOs from their own countries. Developments may be facilitated by serious debate on these questions among NGOs, especially in North-South contexts. Another key to increasing institution-building activities may lie in the ability of official donors to revise their criteria for cofinancing, and to specify appropriate indicators for assessing performance in institution-building.

Indicators of institution-building performance

In 1984, under contract with US AID, Development Alternatives Inc. (DAI) studied the performance of two non-profit US organisations (International Voluntary Service and the Institute for International Development Inc.) in four developing countries. The purpose was to gather insights into the role of local institutions in development and the role of PVOs in building the capacities of local institutions.

On development impact, the study by DAI suggests that the value of an organisation should be measured not just by internal capacity and performance but also by the effect of its activities on the community as a whole and particularly the poor. Studying development impact should include the measuring of effects and benefits in the three areas of economic gain, social benefits and equity effects.

On institutional development, important questions in the study included the scale of indigenous institutions, and the extent to which they were genuinely local. Chances of self-sustaining development increase to the extent that management by local institutions is participatory. This is more often the case with institutions that are small, simple in structure and limited in purpose. In co-operation with a study group of Cornell University, the survey team tested and improved a list of indicators which help measure institutional development outcomes.

The "DAI-Cornell" list of indicators of institutional development is reproduced in an annex to this report (Annex 3). It provides a valuable check-list; and it corresponds to the basic features of institutional development which have emerged from the experience of farmers' groups in West Africa, illustrated in the preceding chapter. A first category of indicators is linked to internal building of capacity: among them, the existence of a system for mediation in conflicts over distribution of resources; staff training programmes, as well as authority to hire, fire and remunerate staff;

and the keeping of records that permit assessment of progress. A second category relates to the building of external "legitimacy", where significant indicators are the forging of horizontal and vertical links by the indigenous organisation, leverage and its advocacy of constituents' interest, etc. A third category includes such indicators as the indigenous organisation's control over resources and its accountablity to constituents for their financial participation. [Development Alternatives Inc., Private Voluntary Organisations and Institutional Development: Lessons from International Voluntary Services, Inc. and the Institute for International Development, prepared under contract for US AID, Washington, 1984.]

A further point which has special relevance to aid donors is the need to modulate financial and technical assistance according to the various stages of development of the supported organisation and to channel some of the aid to support permanent in-country intermediate institutions. This point has already been discussed in Chapter II.

2. DEVELOPMENT IMPACT

Many insights into the developmental impact of host-country self-help organisations are provided by experience from Asian NGOs: a few examples will be drawn from Bangladesh and India. A recent study by Judith Tendler for the Ford Foundation, referred to in a subsequent section, was focused on the common traits of local organisations which have greater impact, most of them in Bangladesh and India.

Experience and strategies of selected Asian self-help NGOs

Bangladesh: BRAC and Grameen Bank

Private voluntary agencies in Bangladesh have been involved in assisting the poor since independence: first in relief and rehabilitation, then health and education. More recently, many NGOs have shifted their emphasis to income generation. In December 1986, 900 NGOs were registered with the Directorate of Social Welfare and 712 with the Directorate of Women's Affairs including many small groups. Some have acquired useful experience, developed successful strategies and are recognised as having brought significant benefits to the poor with whom they work. Several of the largest and most important are domestic NGOs.

A World Bank report on rural employment in Bangladesh, made available to the DAC seminar held in June 1986, concluded that several mainly indigenous NGOs engaged in income-raising and employment-generation become quite effective as contrasted with the poor results of public-sector programmes. It recommended, therefore, that the government should work in close co-operation with these organisations in its rural development programmes. They had developed relevant capacities in organisation and mobilisation of "target" groups, the identification of productive opportunities and the channelling of credit to small rural enterprises and the rural poor. Their constraints included limitations of financial resources and an inadequate capacity to identify investment opportunities and to improve rural technologies. These constraints, the report said, should be removed through provision of training and funding. NGOs selected on the basis of their implementation capacity should be brought into broader strategies for the creation of rural employment.

Amongst several NGOs of recognised interest two are highlighted hereafter. The Bangladesh Rural Advancement Committee is the major NGO in Bangladesh for rural development and the organisation of the landless for economic betterment. It grew from a small relief organisation set up in 1972 to become, by 1982, a body employing 1 500 people. It was by that time helping more than 16 000 families, constituted in 480 groups, with development services and credit for agriculture, fishing, livestock and weaving, and for commercial and marketing activities. BRAC has developed methods for the organisation of village groups through functional literacy and intensive leadership training. It has also more recently launched non-formal primary education and primary health care programmes. But there is a worry that these may detract from its major organisational and income-raising purposes.

BRAC introduced an evaluation system into its operations from the outset. It was led after a few years to recognise that the poor, and women in particular, were not adequately involved, and that its activities were not mutually reinforcing. BRAC accordingly shifted its activities in 1976 to focus entirely on the poorest 50 per cent of village populations. Since 1979, it has organised groups of 20-30 people with similar backgrounds: landless labourers, destitute women, fishermen. The functional literacy programmes use an approach by which group participants are encouraged to analyse their problems and seek solutions. Groups of landless labourers have been organised to lease land, women's groups to undertake paddy processing, and fishermen to buy boats with BRAC providing credit. Initial groups in a village are expected to form other groups, until all the poor in the village are organised. BRAC has developed an "outreach programme" over the past few years, with support from bilateral aid agencies such as Swedish SIDA and foreign NGOs such as Oxfam. BRAC staff identify potential leaders and major concerns of the poor in new areas through an initial survey. As leaders are identified, they learn organisation and motivation methods in BRAC training centres. They then activate group creation by organising functional literacy courses and identifying possible productive activities. Later, the groups apply for resources from BRAC. Loans are extended under group guarantee, at interest rates which may reach up to 30 per cent per annum (traditional money leaders may charge up to 10 per cent per month). Repayment rates are over 95 per cent and household incomes of participants are increased, with high net earnings from activities financed on credit. BRAC also conducts research on the dynamics of rural poverty. In 1983, BRAC was involved in a massive new programme to train rural mothers in oral rehydration techniques for treating diarrhoea. Subsequent foreign aid for further involvement by BRAC in primary health care appears to observers to risk diverting the organisation from its main focus and raison d'être and to call for a review of goals to determine its strategy for the 1990s, choosing between welfare or helping the poor reach self-reliance.

The Grameen Bank was started in 1976 as an experiment in rural finance by a Bangladeshi economist. Formally launched in 1979 with support from the Central Bank of Bangladesh, and registered as a chartered bank in 1983, it is a specialised credit institution for the rural poor. Landless borrowers are majority shareholders: they will ultimately control three-quarters of the bank's paid-up capital. Loans are extended only to the very poor: target groups are families owning less than 0.4 acres of land. To join Grameen, a would-be borrower has to form a group of five. Two members can get loans immediately, but none of the others will get loans unless these group members are repaying regularly. These groups of five people are gender-segregated. Repayments are weekly and groups must regularly save to build up their own capital. Every six groups are federated into centres, typically with one or two centres in each village, meeting weekly to effect repayments and discuss new loan proposals with the bank worker. Branches correspond geographically to the country's lowest administrative unit and comprise 50-60 centres. By December 1986 there were 295 branches, serving over 230 000 members, of whom three-quarters were women. Members' savings totalled $4.6 million. The Bank operated in 5 170 villages in five districts, out of a total of 68 000 villages and 20 districts in Bangladesh. It plans to expand to 500 branches in these five districts by the end of 1988.

Loans have been used primarily for individual agricultural activities, processing and local trading. Approximately 438 000 loans had been extended by 1985 averaging $68 each. Two thirds of individual loans to women have been for paddy husking, purchase of a milch cow or cattle fattening. The leading activity for men has been post-harvest purchase of rice for resale. Average earnings for Grameen's loan recipients have been higher than the national average, per capita incomes have increased, and additional employment has been generated. Repayment rates have been 97 per cent (against an average of 27 per cent for private banks in the country), demonstrating that the poor can use bank credit productively and repay loans on time without collateral guarantees. Interest rates may reach 21 per cent, as against 10 per cent per month and at times per week with moneylenders. The Grameen Bank has more recently also offered loans for housing improvement or construction, with lower interest rates and maturities of 12 to 18 years instead of one year. Equally important is the promotion of social development: members elect yearly the leaders of groups and centres, commit themselves to the discipline of reimbursements and savings, and meet once a week to discuss common problems. In addition, members undertake to respect 16 principles adopted in 1984 on the upkeep of homes, the building of latrines, the planting of trees and vegetables around houses, the abolition of the dowry and of early marriages, the adoption of family planning and preventive health measures etc. [For a concise and clear presentation and assessment, see Maria Nowak, "Une banque pour les pauvres: la Grameen Bank", in Histoires de développement, No. 1, March 1988, Institut d'études sociales de Lyon. A comparative study of four villages in Bangladesh was conducted by a team of Dutch and Bangladeshi social scientists to assess the merits of conscientisation as against the extension of credit as effected by the Grameen Bank: Pieter Streefland (and others), Different Ways to Support the Rural Poor, Effects of Two Development Approaches in Bangladesh, The Hague/Dhaka, the Netherlands Ministry of Development Co-operation, September 1986.]

Like BRAC with its outreach programme, the Grameen Bank has a strategy for developing its activities and stimulating the creation of new groups, by sending young university graduates into rural areas as trainees and then taking them on to its staff. A third of the trainees reportedly do not survive the culture shock, but among those who remain in the villages turnover is low.

An experimental unit was recently created by Grameen Bank to test what enterprises, requiring larger and longer-term loans, could be undertaken by groups of landless men and women [Studies, Innovation, Development and Experimentation (SIDE)]. The Grameen Bank receives support among others from IFAD, the Ford Foundation and German organisations. Substantial aid over a five-year period jointly by IFAD, Norway and Sweden was under consideration in 1986 with the aim of enabling the bank to become self-financing. [Bangladesh Study and Norwegian Aid Review, 1986, The Christian Michelsen Institute, Bergen, 1986.]

India: The Self-Employed Women's Association (SEWA)

Many host-country NGOs are at work in India, alongside foreign NGOs. Indeed, while NGOs of the South generally do not fit into the philanthropic ethos of endowments or fund-raising organisations in the North, India has its own tradition of philanthropic institutions and its voluntary sector has been defined as one of the largest, most diverse and vital to be found anywhere in the world (D. Korten). As early as 1892, the industrialist J.N. Tata established an endowment scheme to fund overseas training for Indian professionals.

One Indian organisation, the comprehensive rural health project of Jamkhed in the state of Maharashtra, was referred to in Chapter II. Based on the Gandhi-inspired movement which encouraged farmers to donate some of their land to the "outcaste" (Harijans), the Association for Sarva Seva Farms (ASSEFA) -- with support from a number of official and private sources, including a special relationship with the Italian NGO Movimento Sviluppo e Pace -- had moved from ten farms developed over 1969-76 and serving 364 families in the state of Tamil Nadu to national significance and activities in eight states involving approximately 100 000 people by 1984 (2). One Indian example, described in detail below, differs from most of the cases already cited in being mainly rooted in urban rather than rural poverty.

SEWA is a registered trade union, founded in 1972 and functioning as the women's wing of the Textile Labour Association of Ahmedabad in the state of Gujarat. It was formed to serve poor women in the informal sector; petty vendors, garment-makers (paid at piece-rates), dealers in used garments, handcart pushers, handloom weavers, waste collectors, firewood gatherers, cigarette rollers, etc. These women are short of capital: a vendor of vegetables does business by borrowing 50 rupees in the morning, and repaying 55 in the evening; the day after, she starts again. They hire their means of production, paying rent for pushcarts, sewing machines. They have no legal protection or social security. For home-based producers, the main problems are the availability of raw material and low piece-rate wages. For vendors, the main problem is obtaining a right to space in the market to avoid being fined and harassed by the police. Because of labour surplus, women who sell various kinds of services or their manual work have no bargaining power: they only work three to five months in the year, at very low wages. SEWA uses occupational groups as its basic organising units to facilitate access to raw materials and markets. It works at securing selling space and requesting fixed or improved wages and pushes policy changes to obtain recognition of self-employment in the informal sector. As a result of SEWA's efforts, the latest five-year plan of India included a separate chapter on self-employment. Although urban-based, SEWA has expanded its trade union and developmental activities into rural areas and become a national-level association. It employed 20 full-time organisers and 100 trade-group leaders in 1987. To provide credit to poor and generally illiterate women, the association established a "SEWA Bank", attracting 13 000 depositors (these receive 6 per cent on their deposits) and, with aid from the government and the Lions' Club, extending part of its loans (normally averaging 12 per cent) at 4 per cent for certain trade groups. SEWA Bank was set up in 1974 to serve as an intermediary between poor women and the nationalised banks, but resorted in 1976 to acting as a co-operative bank on funds of its own (initially $6 000 collected among members and local supporters). By 1986 it had extended loans for a total of $200 000. This is a small sum in absolute terms, whose modesty, together with the indications provided by Dr. Tendler's research (see section below), suggests scope for additional support.

The Mahila SEWA Trust was further established to provide social services for members such as day care, assistance after bereavement, life insurance, maternal benefits and mother-child health programmes. SEWA received support from the government of India and relatively modest foreign assistance from various sources, including Oxfam and the Ford Foundation. In co-operation with several Indian educational and research centres, it carries out surveys and research on local wage structures, occupational health standards, and the design of new tools and equipment for SEWA workers.

Similar problems are faced elsewhere by men and women in the informal sector, including in Africa. An example relates to petty traders, artisans and labourers in Kigali, Rwanda. Action to improve their situation started in 1978, organised by a local Catholic youth movement, until in 1984 they obtained recognition and secured a right to their work places. Joining an association and mobilising resources through savings were part of the process, which was also facilitated by an ILO project for artisans and a Swiss-supported programme to promote local credit-and-savings unions (3). Likewise, the securing of rights for street food vendors in the Sahelian countries was recommended at a recent meeting in Cape Verde referred to in the conclusions of this report.

Traits that favour impact

In 1986, the Ford Foundation initiated a review of its programmes in the area of livelihood, employment, and income-generation (LEIG), a relatively new part of its activities, implemented mainly by NGOs. LEIG addresses the need for increased income and employment among rural poor in off-farm rural occupations, particularly women. Ford Foundation spending on such activities became significant in 1982: over the 1982-86 period, LEIG funding amounted to $21 million, 10 per cent of the total for developing countries. For this review the Foundation chose four of the countries where it has field offices: India, Bangladesh, Kenya and Egypt. [Judith Tendler, What Ever Happened to Poverty Alleviation? A Report Prepared for the Mid-decade Review of the Ford Foundation's Programmes on Livelihood, Employment and Income Generation, 49 pages and annexes, March 1987.] Out of 32 NGOs, institutions and projects visited or studied, the report finds that six have outstanding impact potential. Their beneficiaries are in the thousands. They have grown into competent organisations, recognised by donors as honest, strong, self-criticising and highly capable. They have an influence on policies that affect large numbers of poor people. Five of the six programmes are carried out by NGOs, one by a public-sector enterprise. The NGOs are somewhat special: three are trade unions, one is registered as a bank and one is a private consulting firm. Outstanding performers are: the Grameen Bank of Bangladesh; four women's organisations in India: Self-Employed Women's Association (SEWA) of Ahmedabad, Working Women's Forum (WWF) of Madras, Annapurna Caterers of Bombay, Women's Dairying Project of the Dairy Development Federation of Andhra Pradesh; and a local consulting firm working in conjunction with the association of Zabaleen garbage collectors in Cairo. The study further delineates common traits of outstanding performers. These are: a narrow focus on a particular trade or sector, at least at the beginning; or a narrow focus on one activity, particularly credit, in a "minimalist" form, with little or no evaluation of the intended investment, no technical or business extension, and the burden of selection shifted from the credit entity to peer groups of borrowers themselves; organisational leadership well linked to powerful institutions; and in most cases an urban setting at least at the outset, which allows for agglomeration economies in serving dense populations and a closeness to centres of power.

Their economic activities also share common traits: clients were already producing what they receive assistance for, or new activities were well known in the region and easily mastered; clients' groups were not required to produce collectively or, if they were, managerial and working requirements of the collective operation were minimal; assisted activities did not face competition from large-scale capital-intensive industries; sales markets were already securely in place; supplies of basic inputs were already assured.

To support effective LEIG programmes, therefore, part of the task is to find NGOs whose traits are likely to facilitate expansion. One of these is the ability and willingness to link up to the public sector.

The report draws other lessons from the experience of outstanding organisations. First, concentration on a single task or a particular trade or sector was accompanied by careful studies, carried out by bright and dedicated young generalist staff, who thus gained thorough understanding of the sector or trade and identified possible points of intervention. This led the organisations to incremental approaches: proposing small changes in the way existing things work, through continual study, identification and intervention. Another important feature was that these organisations bargain with authorities for their clients as a group or class, dealing with social issues rather than individual cases. The "minimalist" approach to credit goes hand in hand with requiring savings as a prerequisite to borrowing. "When clients have to save in order to borrow, the organisation will have to first prove that it is a trustworthy place to put one's savings." Also, the organisations providing credit have undergone "a long tutelage of doing no more than working as brokers between their clients and an established bank". That a banking infrastructure existed was crucial to this sequence. Repayment rates to intermediaries constitute a clear and concise measure of their good performance.

On the "urban edge" characteristic of five out of the six cases, Judith Tendler suggests that the spatial dispersion of rural populations and variations in seasonal activities may provide fewer opportunities to work with a single trade or sector. Also, rural-based programmes provide less of a chance to have an influence, as the powerful elites and the powerful institutions are located in large important cities. Experience should then encourage the search for rural strategies that imitate these urban configurations, or compensate for the lack of them. The founder of Grameen Bank focused on providing a "franchisable" service (minimalist credit) that, once perfected, could be applied anywhere throughout the nation, regardless of local conditions. The provision of credit to rural labourers did not antagonise local landowners; nor did the organisation of groups of landless labourers to provide tubewell irrigation, using infrastructure of a defunct public-sector programme. The Grameen Bank was linked from the start to a major centre of national power -- the Central Bank of Bangladesh. The suggestions offered by Judith Tendler's study appear to deserve further reflection and debate, in the search for impact.

3. NGOs' POTENTIAL IN MICRO-POLICY REFORM

To enhance the impact of activities in support of local self-help development another recent paper, by Dr. David Korten, suggests new paths for mature NGOs. [David Korten, "Micro-Policy Reform: The Role of Private Voluntary Development Agencies", Working Paper No. 12 of the National Association of Schools of Public Affairs and Administration, Washington DC, Revised August 1986.] In David Korten's analysis, the need for innovative thinking in private non-profit development agencies, and for expanding their roles, is becoming particularly evident in Asian countries, where financial constraints preclude continued reliance on expensive and wasteful centrally funded and directed public development projects and programmes. For many of these countries, a greater reliance on broadly based local initiatives may be essential. It is important that governments recognise and give effective support to such initiatives, but much of the leadership will need to come from the private sector, in particular from organisations which have acquired relevant expertise.

Macro-policy reforms, such as policies relating to pricing decisions, subsidies and trade policies, can be accomplished through the stroke of an authoritative pen, often with minimal requirements in terms of developing new institutional capacity. In contrast, micro-policy reforms depend on the accomplishment of institutional changes, e.g., the introduction of a credit programme for small farmers where none existed before. Most complex of all may be micro-policy reforms which call for a sharing of power between the national and local levels, and the development of self-reliant participatory organisations. The expertise needed can only be acquired through experience in facilitating processes of institutional change. Performance in micro-policy depends on the exercise of creative initiative by many individuals, so that institutional structures can be rebuilt by persistent action essentially through bottom-up processes. Micro-policy reforms also require careful coalition-building and learning processes. Substantial financial resources and related pressure on spending can actually be a disadvantage. Most people-oriented development activities are micro-policy reforms: these are not implemented by a temporary injection of funds but by changes in attitudes and a better gearing of services and resources to users' needs and demands.

The basis of many micro-policy interventions lies with changing the ways in which existing (rather than additional) resources are controlled and managed. Organisations with modest financial means which see people as the critical development resource are more suited for such tasks. This means that external and domestic development-oriented NGOs, working in developing countries in the thousands, are more likely to act as institutional catalysts than the large donors. But few of them have yet recognised this potential and developed the range of new capacities required to be effective as catalyst organisations. Requirements include experienced professional staff combining in-depth country knowledge, professional credibility, and facilitation skills. Their staff should be relatively free of routine administrative duties, so as to concentrate on problem-centred collegial interaction with counterparts. The organisation must have a capacity to fund quickly and flexibly a range of activities through small grants and contracts as needs and opportunities arise.

An example provided by Dr. Korten relates to the South-East Asia Office of the Ford Foundation in its current support of community-based management of irrigation and forestry resources in Indonesia, the Philippines and Thailand. Ford staff act by stages. They identify key individuals in the major agencies responsible for irrigation and forestry management who are interested in community-based approaches to resource management. They then act as facilitators in action-research processes, playing a key role in agenda setting and providing small grants for experimentation and research. Action-research consists of studies (which are funded by the Foundation but channelled through key individuals in major agencies) of communities' existing resource mangement practices and how they are modified by agencies' programmes. Studies are often carried out by local universities. Findings and implications are examined at workshops at local and national levels by researchers, agency officials and representatives of interested NGOs. These workshops are chaired by senior officials of the responsible agencies and offer opportunities for gradually and continuously expanding the experience base and the number of persons interested. Pilot projects, involving voluntary agencies and social scientists from in-country institutions who assist in the training and supervision of field staff, are conducted to modify the approaches of the agencies in a more participatory direction. Through working groups, lessons are derived from pilot projects for adoption of new approaches by the agencies on a larger scale.

Can other NGOs play a similar role? What would the conditions be? Dr. Korten distinguishes three orientations in NGOs' strategies: a relief and welfare orientation; a local self-reliance orientation; and a "sustainable systems development" orientation. All three co-exist within the larger NGO community and even within a single NGO, and this is appropriate given the diversity of situations they face. The relief and welfare approach of first-generation NGOs remains appropriate in emergency situations and individual welfare assistance. As a development strategy, however, relief and welfare offer little more than temporary alleviation of the symptoms of underdevelopment. A second generation of private development assistance emerged in the 1970s supporting local development activities to promote local self-reliance.

But this second generation is up against a blockage with respect to impact and replication. The fact is that there are still very few recorded cases of good co-operation, based on mutual understanding and a shared perception of the division of responsibilities, between NGOs and government agencies.

Currently, segments of the NGO community are engaged in a re-examination of basic strategic issues such as sustainability, breadth of impact, and recurrent-cost recovery. These third-generation NGOs realise that acting on their own they can never benefit more than a few favoured localities; and that self-reliant village development can be sustained only to the extent that local public and private organisations are linked in a supportive national development system (an "enabling environment") involving many different organisations.

In many instances, first- and second-generation programmes, however necessary, will ultimately prove futile in the absence of a third-generation effort to achieve a policy and institutional setting consistent with their purposes. Third-generation strategies, however, often require the development of the capacities of other collaborating NGOs to meet essential first- and second-generation needs. Awareness of these issues encourages advance from one generation to the next within a given NGO. Can NGOs be helped to evolve a more strategic outlook and a "strategic management" capacity? Current developments in Asia suggest a positive answer. Various Southern and Northern voluntary sector actors have been promoting national and regional NGO encounters on these themes since 1987, favouring the creation of consortium-type bodies, in particular the Asian NGO Coalition (ANGOC) and developing a body of knowledge and methods which can be defined as "strategic" (rather than bureaucratic, control-oriented) management. In liaison with other agencies, the Institute for Development Research (IDR) is developing innovative programmes which deserve mention. IDR is a small private voluntary institution based in Boston. In 1988, it has twice offered to a small number of officials of selected Asian NGOs a kind of sabbatical month, providing opportunities for reflection and study, and for discussing with peers from other countries, leading academics from New England, and decision-makers from US and international aid agencies. These opportunities may be extended in 1989 to NGO leaders from Latin America and Africa in addition to Asia.

Moving from an operational to a catalyst role involves changes in operating style. The NGO will work less as a service-delivery agency. It will be more concerned with facilitating the development in other public and private organisations of the capacities, linkages and commitments required to address designated needs on a sustained basis. It will be able to influence -- not control -- the systems with which it works, with small resources relative to these systems.

The catalytic NGO will aim at improving a target system. This can be a health system, an agricultural production and marketing system, or a credit system. The main role of the catalytic NGO is to facilitate learning by the institutions which compose the system. Some of the organisations involved in the system will be large, influential and staffed by professionals.

Conventional bureaucratic organisations usually respond to needs and opportunities by adding staff and increasing budgets, often leading to costly and partial responses. The strategic organisation's aim, on the contrary, is to increase efficiency in the use of existing resources and better match them with the resources of intended beneficiaries.

Given its aims, and the characteristics of the system which it aims at making more sustainable, the strategic organisation will need to develop several capabilities. The technical competence of its staff must be balanced with social, political and managerial skills, through appropriate recruitment and training and by relationships with centres of technical excellence. It must have in-depth knowledge of the actors and organisations involved, requiring time and experience. It will have to adjust its resources within complex and changing relationships in the social, political and economic context. Since quick results cannot be expected, the third-generation strategy may require the NGO to remain at its task for ten or even twenty years, withstanding critics for whom contributions to development are measured in terms of buildings constructed or numbers of immunisations and of food packages delivered. Capable leaders who combine a long-term vision with highly developed professional management skills are essential.

Steps can be taken for developing the strategic capacity required for third-generation roles. These include sending key senior staff for advanced management training at well established management schools; collaborating with groups which have advanced capabilities in relevant social and policy analysis and its application; recruiting staff with advanced qualifications in social analysis, management, and process facilitation; strengthening internal learning by documenting and critically assessing early third-generation experiences; conducting strategic assessment workshops for senior staff; and participating in exchange of experience with other NGOs which have similar commitments.

Third-generation strategies may require programme specialisation, with a realisation that income generation implies the development of distinctive expertise in a chain of sequences for each activity undertaken, or geographic specialisation, and, when working with governmental services, an adequate recognition of host-country administrative and political jurisdictions. Through a specific programme, an NGO will acquire credibility among persons from a variety of sectors. This credibility represents an important resource. In defining approaches, a third-generation strategy will be mindful of impact: while a second-generation strategy is directed to building capacities in individual communities to meet their needs through self-reliant action, a third-generation strategy will concentrate on reorienting supportive systems and policies so that they strengthen the capacity of many communities to address identified needs.

4. IMPROVING AID FOR SUPPORT INSTITUTIONS: A CONTRIBUTION BY CEBEMO

Dr. Koenraad Verhagen has recently completed a study for the Dutch NGO CEBEMO, in the wake of action-research by the German special unit "ES 31" (see Chapter II) and building on CEBEMO's own experience. The purpose of the study is to enlarge donor perceptions on how to go about promoting self-help by better assessing the role of support institutions. [Koenraad Verhagen, Self-Help Promotion: A Challenge to the NGO Community, CEBEMO -- Royal Tropical Institute, Amsterdam, 1987.] The study validates indications from other research and recommends changes in priorities, away from the concern with quick absorption of donor money.

Three cases were investigated, in Brazil, Indonesia and Thailand, and "self-assessments" were conducted with project teams in each case. In Brazil, the study focused on the rural side of a broad programme involving economic activities in rural areas, primary health care, support for rural trade unions, and small-scale urban programmes; in Indonesia, the organisation (Bina Swadaya) promotes savings and credit in "pre-co-operative" form, also undertaking income-generating activities; in Thailand, social-action centres successfully promote many varied activities in villages. The conclusions again underline the inconsistency of the project approach with self-help promotion requirements. Donor NGOs in their partnership with support institutions operate under a number of constraints -- some are of their own making -- leaving inadequate time to develop clear and comprehensive strategies for self-help promotion. Several "tools" require more persistent attention:

-- Identification of the poor, especially when activities centre upon economic issues;

-- Participatory research and planning, preventing the risk of encouraging activities beyond local management capacity;

-- Education and mutual training, especially two-way processes of knowledge-sharing and generation, such as in village gatherings;

-- Mobilisation of local resources, often inhibited by the "spending pressure" of large foreign aid organisations;

-- Proper monitoring of financial performance with suitable book-keeping systems and attention to depreciation of donor-financed assets and to hidden subsidies;

-- Concentration on small areas and selected "core" or "mentor" villages, rather than a scattered "butterfly" approach;

-- Facilitating linkages, so that local groups can approach the governmental and non-governmental agencies which can best secure their interests in given fields;

-- More regular and systematic assessments of strategies, working methods and performance, and strengthening in-built feedback mechanisms which at present do not exist or do not function properly.

Support institutions currently devote much time and energy to a role they should probably not play: acting as intermediaries in the flow of resources from donor agencies to local groups. This leaves them little time for their own catalytic and supportive roles. The study therefore recommends a clear separation between banking and promotional functions.

The scale of the study does not warrant definitive conclusions on typical features of effective support institutions. Some indications suggest that effectiveness is probably greatest when the organisation is small; its staff (10-20 people) can work as a single team at (sub-)regional level; it has a high degree of autonomy in deciding its policies but forms part of a self-reinforcing network of support institutions.

A crucial problem, not always recognised by foreign donors, is the financial sustainability of support institutions. "Since it is difficult to make money out of the poor, projects have to be undertaken and maintained which generate income;" but these may imply working with a more affluent clientele. The alternative course, of working exclusively with the poor, leaves the support institution dependent on foreign aid. The study has no solutions to offer at this stage.

Finally, the CEBEMO study recommends that much more attention be paid to the development of a methodology for self-help promotion, putting a brake on external donors' frequent activism and their eagerness to fund tangible projects with quick implementation. The study is currently used within CEBEMO for discussing desirable changes in policy and in the forms of its financial relations with partner institutions in developing countries. The scope of the discussion has been further enlarged, to include other agencies in the Netherlands and internationally, beginning with a conference in the Netherlands in October 1987 (CEBEMO, Report on the Proceedings of the Expert Consultation on Promotion of Autonomous Development, October 1987).

5. SELF-EVALUATION IN LOCAL ORGANISATIONS

As has been mentioned in the preceding section, the CEBEMO study was based on "self-assessments" conducted together with project teams in the three cases investigated. Experience with self-help groups, and the interest of some evaluators in specific features of small projects, is resulting in the development of various methods of "self-evaluation", one of which is described below in some detail. The interest in self-evaluation is in part an answer to the question of who should evaluate "small projects" and self-help groups, and to what purpose. To what extent does exploring whether income-generating activities are set on the right course, intended beneficiaries actually benefit, etc., warrant professional external evaluations? Another reason for having recourse to self-assessments is that evaluation is coming to be seen as a permanent internal management tool, to which beneficiaries should be associated. The evaluation conducted for the Commission of the European Communities in 1985 and summarised in Chapter V quotes the example of a project in Latin America where a host-country professional (a sociologist) comes periodically and holds self-evaluation sessions with project operators and local group members. It recommends extending this practice.

A similar conclusion was reached by a group of professionals from French NGOs which met throughout 1985-86 to work on the question of criteria for the evaluation of small projects. The results of this work have been published recently and several points appear to deserve mention (4). In the first place, existing evaluation methods, even though some may be more suited to small projects than others, remain alien to the intended beneficiaries at grass-roots level and unsuited to representing their viewpoint.

Another major and frequent difficulty is the lack of basic accounting data, mainly because of the lack of accounting skills among local project operators. In financial evaluations, amortization is almost never taken into account, nor other hidden costs. Some of the inputs and outputs do not have a market value: for example, voluntary work contributed by intended beneficiaries, greater availability of food for household consumption, or gains in time obtained through new agricultural practices and new technology. Some project results, such as greater group cohesion or self-confidence, are not of an economic nature. A major practical problem is the high cost of evaluations relative to the total cost of individual projects, many of them below $15 000 in the experience of French NGOs.

For small projects of local groups the research team recommends more frequent adoption of methods of guided self-evaluation (auto-évaluation animée) which can develop from a simple consultation into a permanent management feature. The team refers to one particular method of self-evaluation developed by Paul Willot of Belgium (5). Preparatory work for guided self-evaluations conducted according to this method starts well in advance, by correspondence, asking questions such as "what is the purpose of the evaluation?", or "what is the duration of the project?" rather than requesting data. In effect, it is usually discovered on the spot that many of the data requested are needless, and many of those needed are not available. The method was derived from the "logical framework" but transformed into a participatory tool. Provision is made for deducing goals from activities and for defining indicators together with the group: the exercise in the field starts by defining who does what and how it is done. There follows the identification of means available to the group or team, unit costs, intended or implied goals and activities to be evaluated. The analysis of results leads to the definition of quantitative and qualitative indicators. The first stage, where the animateur works together with the project team, usually lasts one week. During a second stage, usually of two weeks' duration, the project team applies the measurements agreed upon while the beneficiary population is asked by the animateur for its own appreciation of the project. A third stage of one week is needed to establish permanent evaluation activities: elaborating a calendar and indicators for the various projects, defining who will be responsible and deciding on further training needs so that self-evaluation can continue with no external guidance. The various stages may take place separately over time. Project operators tend to be strongly critical of their own action while beneficiary populations feel more closely involved as a result of this exercise. Many self-evaluations of this kind have been conducted in various African countries.

Self-evaluation gradually comes to be recognised as an important tool for building awareness, self-confidence and participatory management in local organisations, permitting the development of other approaches chosen by the community itself. For these purposes, self-evaluation cannot be done on a one-off basis, as tends to be the case with external evaluations, but must be pursued continuously as an integral part of the process of development.

6. APPROPRIATE TECHNOLOGY

NGOs most frequently have to deal with questions of appropriate or inappropriate technology in two ways: either they need to solve a specific problem, seeking the specialised knowledge required, or technology choices are made at national level which modify the employment and income options of the people with whom they work. Subsidiary points include the often slow pace at which promising prototypes get to be produced locally on a larger scale, which may reflect an inadequate commitment of the donor agencies involved, and the particular problem, in the context of the African focus of this report, of the technological neglect of the Sahel. In many cases, neglect of appropriate technology may have an even larger impact on women than on men.

Project operators or local group leaders are often faced with a technological problem. For example, the European Consortium for Agricultural Development (ECAD), formed by CCFD, CEBEMO, Deutsche Welthungerhilfe and Mani Tese, noticed in an agricultural project in Cambodia that maize was locally hand-thrashed, damaging the grains with loss of produce. A small factory manufacturing simple machines for dehusking maize was identified in Padua and 70 such machines were bought. Requirements, however, are for 5 000. ECAD will now stimulate in-country production by small workshops and blacksmiths.

The NGO ACORD has a significant record in training local skills, for example for installing, maintaining and repairing water pumps in Rwanda, and is planning assistance to blacksmiths in Ethiopia for local production of agricultural tools. Local potential is often entirely bypassed by larger programmes funding the installation of, for example, thousands of pumps at once.

A number of specialised appropriate technology agencies exist in developed and developing countries, some of them NGOs, others fully financed by the public sector, providing assistance on request. In 1980, an international appropriate technology network, Socially Appropriate Technology International Information Services (SATIS), was established, which now groups 41 such agencies (6). Its secretariat is hosted by the Royal Tropical Institute in Amsterdam.

Examples given by specialists of appropriate technology developed on a large scale include the practical applications of the discovery of oral rehydration, beginning to be widely adopted through efforts by UNICEF, US AID and others; tens of thousands of hand-thrashers in use in Thailand and the Philippines and half a million manually operated pumps which have increased the productivity and improved the health of at least a million people in Bangladesh (7). But the granting of importing licenses for capital-intensive equipment, at times in the framework of bilateral and multilateral aid projects, often displaces the activities of millions of villagers, in many cases women, extending absolute poverty. The World Bank report on employment issues in rural development in Bangladesh mentioned earlier in this chapter provides several examples, noting additionally that the capital-intensive imported equipment often works at very reduced capacity. Technology choices form part of broader strategies whose implications are not always fully realised at the outset. The most ingenious efforts of local and foreign NGOs for the creation of rural employment can be rendered insignificant by the scale of disruption which administrative decisions can cause.

A special plea was made at the DAC seminar held in June 1986 for more investment by donors in appropriate technology and appropriate training for women in Sub-Saharan Africa, both to reduce their work burden and to enhance income generation. When more advanced technology is introduced, it often drives women out of a remunerative task which was traditionally reserved for women: e.g., hand machines for the extraction of palm oil, which require a physical strength which most women do not have. Prototypes may be developed to suit women's capacity but are often not followed up by general production.

Women's participation in local self-help groups may result in more attention to their requirements, as witnessed by the spread of millet mills in such groups in West Africa.

There is a grim reminder of the neglect of technology in Sahelian countries, the wheel. Carts, hand-carts and pulleys to help draw water from wells all require the wheel. More widespread use of the wheel would reduce the burden on men and women, more particularly women, as it is they who carry produce from the field to the village, from the village to the market place, and fetch water and firewood. René Dumont reminds us of this simple fact, which has escaped the notice so far, for instance, of thousands of technicians at various levels who have been involved in installing wells over the past three decades (8).

7. FOSTERING SMALL ENTERPRISE IN THE INFORMAL SECTOR

In 1978-84, US AID funded a "Programme for Investment in the Small Capital Enterprise Sector" (PISCES) to explore the feasibility of direct assistance to informal sector micro-enterprises. Building on the experience of the first few years, demonstration projects were designed, implemented and evaluated in four countries. Four case studies were subsequently undertaken. [The Pisces II Experience: vol. I, Local Efforts in Micro-Enterprise Development, vol. II, Case Studies from Dominican Republic, Costa Rica, Kenya and Egypt, US AID, Washington, 1985.] The case studies relate to assistance by the American NGO Accion to the Dominican Development Foundation, and direct or counterpart-funded assistance by US AID for small business schemes run by the National Council of Churches in Kenya, the Coptic Evangelical Organisation for Social Services in Egypt, and the Popular Community Development Bank in Costa Rica. At the same time, one in a series of AID reports dealing with the role of NGOs in the development of small-scale enterprises developed an ex post benefit-cost analysis constructing benefit estimates for five relevant NGO projects. [P. Kilby and D. D'Zmura, Wesleyan University, Searching for Benefits, AID Special Study No. 28, June 1985. The cases studies are: the Partnership for Productivity Project in Upper Volta, now Burkina Faso; the North-Eastern Union of Assistance to Small Business (UNO) Programme in Brazil; the Institute for Honduran Development Programme in Honduras; the Dominican Development Foundation Projects in the Dominican Republic; the Rural Development Fund Programme in Peru.]

These studies enlarge our knowledge and understanding of the processes and difficulties of implementing micro-enterprise projects that reach the poorest strata of the population. In addition, Searching for Benefits also represents a rare example of calculation of benefit-cost ratios for such projects. Its main conclusions can be summarised as follows. The major development problem for small business (defined as micro-enterprise in the informal sector, at family household level) is lack of capital, particularly of working credit. Technical assistance, in terms of supplying advice on management and technical know-how, is largely insignificant in the promotion of small business in the traditional informal sector, but adds significantly to costs. Very simple loan systems are the most cost-effective. For a number of reasons including their own low costs, NGOs should have a potential comparative advantage in the promotion of micro-enterprise.

Important conclusions of PISCES II relate to new directions and implications for donors. New directions should:

-- Institutionalise the capacity to reach the informal sector; at present every micro-enterprise project is "hand-built" and the same mistakes are often repeated;

-- Scale up projects and lower their costs; the best efforts documented by PISCES reached less than one per cent of their potential beneficiaries.

The conclusion is that donors should assist and facilitate the development of institutional capacity on a much larger scale, so that local organisations can support much larger numbers of micro-enterprises in the informal sector. Donors should also encourage policy changes that promote the informal sector rather than being adverse to it as is often the case. Positive changes would include simplified licensing procedures, access to credit, equitable prices for raw materials and support for institutions that can deliver credit at the community level.

8. TRIANGULAR OPERATIONS

Some NGOs are now involved in "triangular operations" in Sub-Saharan African countries whereby a funding donor provides cash -- rather than food aid -- for the purchase and transport of food items from a neighbouring country, or a surplus area within the country concerned. This is in response to situations where the delayed arrival of food aid after the 1984-85 emergency was disruptive for local small farmers in areas where local harvests had been good, to the point that they could not sell their produce -- a situation which in some Sahel countries continues to this day. An example is provided by the "Afrique verte" ("Green Africa") campaign of three French NGOs, Frères des hommes, Terre des hommes, and Peuples solidaires. The campaign promoted "triangular operations" of this kind which it helped to fund, also receiving official support, mainly from the European Commission (CEC) and France. Operations were conducted in liaison with partner farmers' organisations in the recipient countries. In Zaire, a first transfer of 190 tons of dried fish was effected in 1985 by "Solidarité paysanne" from North to South Kivu. In 1986, this was increased to 1 450 tons of rice, dried fish and beans, with other local NGOs also involved. In Senegal, a test was made in 1985 by Terre des hommes and repeated in 1986, in co-operation with an association grouping 26 villages. In Burkina Faso, the organising group effected its purchases using its own funds as well as French aid in the form of a revolving fund, but it found that its management and storage capacity did not enable it to exceed 1 000 tons. These are very small amounts compared with requirements and organisers recognise that more experience is required by the NGOs and local associations involved. They believe, however, that the publicity given to food self-sufficiency goals, in Senegal in particular, was an important result. It may also have contributed to "triangular operations" undertaken by several bilateral donors on a much larger scale. The CEC likewise adopted regulations for funding food purchases: on its 1986 budget, 10 million ECU were earmarked for developing-country governments' requests, and 3 million ECU for similar operations managed by NGOs.

9. NEW FINANCIAL TOOLS OF NGOs

Funding by external NGOs is usually done by extending grants. Currently, however, as an outcome of their growing interest in supporting income-raising activities a number of European NGOs are experimenting with the extension of credit guarantees against hard currency bank deposits, and, in France in particular, investment funds to support small productive projects. Factual information on recent examples is provided hereafter. Examples are the Recherches et applications de financements alternatifs au développement (RAFAD), a foundation in Geneva, the Société d'investissement et de développement international (SIDI) and "Epargne sans frontières" in Paris, the SCOD Bank (Co-operative Society of Mutual Help for Development) in the Netherlands. RAFAD extends credit guarantees to groups or associations through the regular bank system and aims at providing credit to partners rather than projects. SIDI was founded by the French Catholic NGO CCFD with a capital of FF 10 million for direct investment and credit for small enterprises. In 1986, it was reorienting its activities to promote the creation of investment companies in developing countries in association with local banks among others. Started in 1983 by CCFD and later joined by four other French NGOs, the "Fonds commun de placement Faim et Développement" is an investment fund managed by a co-operative bank. Subscribers agree to donate to one of the associated NGOs the difference between annual yields (deposits are mainly invested in bonds) and the inflation rate (9). These amounts are mainly invested by the NGOs in equity participations in small enterprises in developing countries.

Women's World Banking, an independent, non-profit international organisation incorporated in the Netherlands and with operating headquarters in New York, became operational in 1980. Its main goal is to promote the entrepreneurship of women, particularly women who would not otherwise have access to credit. It operates as a financial institution extending loan guarantees to banks and providing technical and management advice to direct and indirect beneficiaries of guarantees. Beneficiaries must be supported by a local affiliate group, usually a women's organisation, working with WWB. With contributions from various official and private sources and the sale of debentures, WWB capital fund neared $2 million by 1984. The letters of credit against dollar deposits have a leverage effect on the size of the local-currency loan. WWB affiliates are active in some fifty countries, most of them developing, and include SEWA in India and the Kenya Women's Finance Trust in Nairobi.

Contacts are maintained between NGOs from several European countries involved in these recent developments, some of which may be considered to be at an experimental stage, and discussions have been inititated with official donors to consider whether they could contribute, in particular, to the funds against which credit guarantees are extended to small entrepreneurs and self-help groups in developing countries.

NOTES AND REFERENCES

1. Initial findings fom Brian Smith's study, published in Gorman, op. cit., are quoted in Chapter I.

2. See An Introduction to ASSEFA and An Approach to Development. Some ASSEFA Experiences (1986), available in Europe at the Fondation Vaujana, Pully, Switzerland.

3. See B. Lecomte, C. Maldonado, P. Ransoni, "La promotion du 'secteur non structuré' : Le cas de Kigali", in Revue Tiers monde, XXVII, No. 106, April-June 1986, Presses universitaires de France.

4. Alain Lalau-Keraly and Geneviève Prady, Les petits projets et l'évaluation, une question d'angle de vue, AMIRA, brochure No. 53, September 1987.

5. Paul Willot, CRID-Belgique.

6. SATIS publishes a Catalogue of Publications, whose 3rd edition, in 1986, presented an annotated bibliography of 865 appropriate technology publications in English, French and Spanish.

7. See among others Frances Stewart in Issues in Science and Technology, vol. III, No. 4, Summer 1987, National Academy of Science, Washington DC.

8. René Dumont, "Le danger démographique", in Le Monde diplomatique, July 1987.

9. By mid-1986, deposits exceeded FF 100 million ($14.4 million), with donations to the NGOs of almost FF 14 million ($2 million).

Chapter IV

OFFICIAL AGENCIES' CO-OPERATION WITH NGOs

Aid agency co-operation with NGOs may include forms of institutional dialogue covering all aspects of development co-operation policy. This is the case of a few DAC Members. In a few others, there are mechanisms for involving NGOs or even granting them major responsibility in the allocation of official contributions to NGOs. All DAC Members give financial support to NGOs. Criteria and coefficients vary considerably. The classical form of financial co-operation is the "matching grant". Several DAC Members have adopted streamlining procedures to reduce the administrative burden of processing a great number of individual NGO projects, by adopting "block grants" or by channelling the bulk of their contributions to a limited number of major and experienced NGOs or through NGO umbrella organisations. Evaluations summarised in Chapter V indicate that official support for evaluations and feasibility studies could usefully be raised in a number of DAC countries to enhance the quality of NGO work. Some aid agencies also contract NGOs as implementors of official-sector activities. In recent years, several DAC Members have developed ways for providing aid-agency support to NGOs of the South, from headquarters, or through in-country funds. Many agencies of the UN system co-operate formally or informally with NGOs. UNDP is establishing a system of grants for NGOs in developing countries, and UNHCR often contracts NGOs to implement programmes for refugees. The World Bank has provided information on its co-operation with NGOs in rural areas in Sub-Saharan Africa, through contracts and consultations, also summarised in this chapter. At the NGO/World Bank Committee, a dialogue is under way on some of the most difficult issues affecting the poor in developing countries, notably debt and structural adjustment. Among regional development banks, the Asian Development Bank was the first, in July 1987, to establish procedures for formal co-operation with NGOs.

1. DAC MEMBERS

Fostering the dialogue between official donors and NGOs

The Scandinavian countries have long had mechanisms for consulting with their national NGOs on official aid policies. In Sweden NGOs form part of the political and administrative system. They are represented in SIDA's Board and participate to some extent in the formulation and implementation of Swedish aid policy. Various other advisory or governing bodies of the official aid programme include representatives of NGOs whose views are regularly called for at all stages in planning, administration and policy-making. A similar co-operative relationship exists between DANIDA and the NGO community in Denmark thanks to the permanent system of consultation built into the government administration responsible for development assistance. For example, the nine members of DANIDA's Advisory Board, which meets once a month to discuss projects, are appointed by various private associations including NGOs. In order further to extend its co-operation with Norwegian NGOs, NORAD has introduced meetings twice a year allowing for discussion of problems and topical issues as well as exchange of information.

In some other DAC countries, there is no formal mechanism for a dialogue on official aid policies but NGOs are institutionally involved by the government in decisions affecting aid-agency cofinancing with NGOs. The Joint Financing Scheme of the Netherlands has already been mentioned. In Australia, this role is played by the Committee for Development Co-operation, which involves the government and the national NGO council, the Australian Council for Overseas Aid (ACFOA), established in 1965. The Committee for Development Co-operation is composed of three nominees each from the government and ACFOA. It advises the government on the development of policy of the cofinancing programme and its operation and makes recommendations on the eligibility of organisations, the allocation of funds and the approval of project submissions. In Germany, periodic meetings are held between the Ministry for Economic Co-operation and NGOs of the major groupings (Catholic, Protestant and non-denominational) for consultations allowing for flexible adaptation of procedures to the commonly recognised requirements of NGO development co-operation.

Over the past few years, French NGOs have established loose umbrella organisations ("collectifs") which now group almost all the agencies of national significance. Concurrently, in 1983 France introduced a new administrative structure with the ultimate purpose of integrating NGOs more formally within the national development co-operation policy, the "Commission Coopération Développement", composed of government and NGO representatives. The Commission aims at facilitating dialogue and aid co-ordination between French authorities and NGOs, enabling NGOs to be more aware of official aid policies, while government officials have an opportunity to become better acquainted with NGOs' approaches and concerns.

A distinct change in New Zealand's NGOs' attitudes and their relationships with the government has occurred since 1985, when major voluntary agencies established the Council for International Development (CID). CID currently has 21 affiliated agencies and has taken a more active approach to development issues and government policy, especially on ODA volume and targets. In Japan, the Japanese NGO Centre for International Co-operation was established in 1987 to promote growth and mutual co-operation among NGOs and a dialogue between NGOs and the government. In 1988, this Centre published a directory of Japanese NGOs, providing factual information on their resources, expenditures and activities (see reference under Chapter I).

The EEC/NGO Liaison Committee established at the Commission of the European Communities, in addition to being an institutionalised opportunity for contact among an estimated 600 European NGOs, also enables a continuing dialogue with the Commission and, more recently, with the European Parliament, notably its committee on development and co-operation.

Within the OECD's Development Assistance Committee itself, a discussion between representatives of official aid agencies and NGOs is planned for 1988 on desirable procedural changes towards the strengthening of NGO partners in developing countries, on the basis of a study contributed by a Member country.

Volume of NGO grants and official contributions

In the past ten years NGOs' activities have increased impressively and have become a significant element in development co-operation. At present over 4 000 NGOs mobilise financial and human resources in DAC Member countries for projects they operate directly or in partnership with countless groups and associations in developing countries.

In 1985 over $4.5 billion in NGO support was granted to developing countries equivalent to about 15 per cent of total official development assistance. Two thirds of this amount or $2.9 billion constituted grants funded by NGOs themselves. The remaining one third or $1.6 billion was matching contributions from DAC governments. By 1986, the total had risen to $5.3 billion, of which $3.3 billion made up of grants by NGOs themselves (see Table IV-1A for data on 1985, and Table IV-1B for 1986).

Grants from NGOs' own resources

NGOs' capacity to raise private resources for development aid varies widely from country to country. Given fluctuations in exchange rates, this is best expressed by the share of NGO grants in countries' gross national product. Ireland had the highest ratio in 1985, at 0.13 per cent, followed by the Netherlands, Norway and Sweden (0.08 per cent), against a DAC average of 0.03 per cent.

Little is known about the reasons for the large differences between DAC Members in the relative importance of private grants but factors such as a tradition of private voluntary involvement with problems of society undoubtedly play an important role. A marked increase in NGO grants in Japan, from $41 million in 1984 to $101 million in 1985, reflected strong support by the public for aid to Africa.

Expressed in 1986 prices and exchange rates, private support for NGO operations increased by almost $1 billion between 1975-76 and 1985-86. In relative terms, however, its share in GNP for DAC countries combined remained constant at 0.03 per cent. These averages mask variations in individual DAC countries: the ratio to GNP increased over time in several countries, e.g., Finland, the Netherlands, Norway, Sweden and the United States.

Table IV-1A

RESOURCES FOR DEVELOPMENT AND RELIEF ACTIVITIES
OF NON-GOVERNMENTAL ORGANISATIONS, 1985

	Private grants extended by NGOs		Official contributions to NGOs (a)	
	US$ million equivalent	$ per capita	US$ million equivalent (b)	Percentage of total ODA
Australia	52	3.30	13	1.7
Austria	18	2.38	1	0.4
Belgium	23	2.33	27	6.1
Canada	171	6.74	129	7.9
Denmark	16	3.13	7	1.6
Finland	13	2.65	4	1.9
France	65	1.18	43	1.1
Germany	424	6.95	174	5.9
Ireland	22	6.18	2	5.1
Italy	8	0.14	39	3.6
Japan	101	0.84	41	1.1
Netherlands	98	6.77	69	6.1
New Zealand	8	2.46	1	1.9
Norway	52	12.54	34	5.9
Sweden	78	9.34	33	3.9
Switzerland	54	8.27	41 (c)	13.6
United Kingdom	169	2.98	13	0.8
United States	1 513	6.32	803 (d)	8.5
Total DAC countries	2 884	4.13	1 473 (e)	5.0

a. Excludes contributions to international voluntary agencies.
b. In most cases, contributions for private volunteer schemes are included, as are contracts with NGOs for the implementation of official projects.
c. Includes subcontracting of NGOs.
d. Fiscal year. Includes $327 million related to food aid, excludes an additional $243 million for emergency programmes administered by PVOs. Also includes subcontracting of PVOs in addition to matching grants.
e. In addition, the Commission of the European Communities contributed $29 million for cofinancing NGO projects (and, additionally, $45 million for food aid and $35 million for emergency aid channelled through NGOs).

Source: Members' submissions to the DAC.

Table IV-1B

RESOURCES FOR DEVELOPMENT AND RELIEF ACTIVITIES
OF NON-GOVERNMENTAL ORGANISATIONS, 1986

	Private grants extended by NGOs		Official contributions to NGOs (a)	
	US$ million equivalent	$ per capita	US$ million equivalent (b)	Percentage of total ODA
Australia	40	2.50	5	0.7
Austria	19	2.51	2	1.0
Belgium	23	2.33	36	6.6
Canada	176	6.86	168	9.9
Denmark	12	2.34	..	..
Finland	28	5.69	8	2.6
France	84	1.52	17	0.3
Germany	545	8.92	248	6.5
Ireland	20	5.63	3	4.8
Italy	11	0.19	42	1.8
Japan	82	0.66	92	1.6
Netherlands	140	9.61	112	6.4
New Zealand	7	2.13	1	1.3
Norway	57	13.67	49	6.1
Sweden	85	10.16	37	3.4
Switzerland	66	10.04	59 (c)	14.0
United Kingdom	191	3.37	12	0.7
United States	1 753	7.26	1 060 (d)	11.1
Total DAC countries	3 338	4.75	1 951 (e)	5.3

a. Excludes contributions to international voluntary agencies.
b. In most cases contributions for private volunteer schemes are included, as are contracts with NGOs for the implementation of official projects.
c. Includes $34.2 million contracts and $19.6 million matching grants.
d. Fiscal year. Includes $354.2 million related to food aid, includes an additional $168.1 million for emergency aid administered by PVOs: for previous years, such emergency programmes were excluded. Also includes sub-contracting of PVOs in addition to matching grants.
e. In addition, the Commission of the European Communities contributed $48.7 million for cofinancing NGO projects (and, additionally, $59 million for food aid, $15 million for emergency aid, and $7 million for aid to refugees, aid to the people of Chile and the purchase of food products by NGOs).

Source: Members' submissions to the DAC.

Official contributions to NGOs

Official contributions to supplement these private resources have increased substantially over the past ten years and in 1985 accounted for 5 per cent of total ODA provided by DAC Members. This trend indicates the recognition by governments of the increasing value to them of co-operating with NGOs and the importance attached by aid agencies to poverty alleviation programmes at the grass-roots level. The volume of funds provided in support for NGOs and their share in total ODA vary considerably between DAC countries, as shown by Table IV-1. Funding is extended for activities in developing countries and, to a lesser degree, also for development education activities conducted by NGOs in DAC countries. In Germany, 8.5 per cent of the budget of the Ministry of Economic Co-operation was channelled to NGOs in 1986 (1).

Target shares in aid

Only one DAC Member so far, the United States, has established targets for the share of aid funds allocated to NGOs. These targets have been in existence for many years, on the basis of legislative mandates, for food aid provided on a grant basis under Title II of Public Law 480 of the Agricultural Trade and Development Act of 1954. Title II relates to food aid provided through PVOs, FAO, the World Food Programme and various government-to-government programmes designed to benefit needy people directly. These grants cover both the cost of commodities and a substantial part of transport costs. The three major categories are food for work, maternal and child health, and school feeding, all targeted to vulnerable groups. Within a proposed programme level for fiscal year 1988 of $535 million for Title II food aid (including $196.3 million for ocean transportation and overland delivery to land-locked countries), the legislated "minimum" for development activities of voluntary agencies is of 1.4 million metric tons, in a total of 1.9 million metric tons. In addition, voluntary agencies have access to the smaller amounts of food surpluses made available on a grant basis by Section 416 of the Agricultural Act of 1949. These amounts mainly relate to dairy products. They vary from year to year and are not allocated on a targeted basis. AID encourages PVOs to establish well-targeted, multi-year programmes for Title II food aid, and to monetise Title II and Section 416 commodities as a source of local currency when required for transport, storage and complementary inputs.

More recently, targets have also been established for other forms of aid. In 1981, Congress required that a minimum amount equal to 12 per cent (with a target of 16 per cent) of AID's development assistance programme budget be channelled through PVOs, including co-operatives. The minimum target was raised to 13.5 per cent for each of fiscal years 1986 through 1989.

Although not mandated by legislative targets, through planned increases in official cofinancing approximately 20 per cent of the bilateral development co-operation budget of Sweden is expected to be allocated to NGOs during fiscal year 1987/88, including emergency aid.

Forms of financial co-operation

Cofinancing schemes in support of NGO projects

All DAC Members have developed systems for cofinancing NGO projects and have adjusted procedures over the years to respond better to requirements. The sections below compare features of general interest in various current cofinancing schemes.

Matching grants for the financing of individual projects

In its original and classical form the cofinancing procedure used by all DAC members is the matching grant by which the government supplements the financing of an NGO project on condition that the NGO itself contributes an agreed share of the needed funds from its own resources, demonstrating its ability to mobilise private support for its development activities. Typical ratios in cofinancing are shown in Table IV-2.

Variations in ratios applied may be used to encourage NGOs to increase their activities in certain sectors or developing countries, as indicated by footnotes to Table IV-2. They may also be used to encourage certain types of donations. A particular case is Canada's present policy of trying to match individual NGOs' fund-raising on a one-to-one basis, whereas official contributions for specific projects overseas may reach a three-to-one ratio. Germany may raise its contribution to 100 per cent in the case of specially important projects in the least developed countries. Other DAC countries likewise modulate their upper limit (see footnotes to Table IV-2).

Exactness in requirements concerning the origin and precise amount of the share of project costs not funded by the aid agency varies considerably between DAC Members. In some countries, the requirement can be applied flexibly and the NGO share may in fact be covered by other funding sources or even be represented by the estimated value of counterpart contributions in developing countries.

Initially, matching grants were allocated on a project-by-project basis for a period of one year, corresponding to the annual budget of aid agencies, sometimes with a commitment for financial support over two to three years. After years of practice, this procedure is now considered to have drawbacks both for the aid agency and the recipient NGO.

For an aid agency, the approval of individual and often small projects raises administrative problems in terms of time and staff as the number of projects submitted by NGOs keeps increasing. Adequate staff is the key to timely processing of project requests: the recent evaluations in Finland and Sweden mentioned in Chapter V recommended an increase in aid agency staff assigned to NGOs as a pre-condition to reaching desired increases in official cofinancing. By way of example, CIDA's NGO Division increased from a staff of five in 1968 to 30 person/years in 1982, when it cofinanced over 2 000 NGO projects and dealt with about 200 NGOs. It still counted 30 persons in 1987, when the number of projects was 3 500 and disbursements had risen to roughly $100 million from about $45 million in 1982.

Table IV-2

COEFFICIENTS GENERALLY PRACTISED BY DAC COUNTRIES FOR OFFICIAL
CONTRIBUTIONS TO NGO PROJECTS

As a general rule	Members
50 per cent	Australia (a), France, New Zealand (b), Switzerland (c), United Kingdom (d), United States (e), CEC
60 per cent	Finland
75 per cent	Belgium, Germany, Ireland
80 per cent	Norway (f), Sweden (g)
100 per cent	Denmark, Netherlands
No fixed percentage	Canada (h), Italy (i), Japan

a. Australia: may be raised to 75 per cent for Pacific countries and LLDCs.
b. A higher subsidy rate of 3:1 is granted by New Zealand for projects which expand women's development opportunities.
c. Switzerland: may be raised to 66 per cent.
d. United Kingdom: percentages may be raised under special circumstances, reaching 100 per cent for population projects.
e. United States: grants allocated by US aid missions may reach 75 per cent. In practice though US PVOs are currently expected to fund 20 per cent of the costs.
f. Norway: in addition, 3 per cent of total documented operational costs may be granted towards administrative costs.
g. Sweden: projects for handicapped people may be cofinanced up to 90 per cent.
h. Canada: matching ratios granted by CIDA vary from 50 per cent for fund-raising NGOs to 100 per cent for universities, professional organisations, volunteer-sending organisations, etc.
i. Italy: up to 70 per cent for the cofinancing of NGO projects.

NGO programmes need a longer-term assurance of financing and greater flexibility in the use of funds than is usually allowed for by matching grants for specific projects.

In order to ease these constraints, a number of aid agencies have devised ways: 1) to move beyond the project-by-project procedure to cover simultaneously several projects through block grants and, in some DAC countries, to confine support to a limited number of NGOs; and, 2) to expand the time frame of their support through various types of multi-year funding procedures.

Block grants

Block grants cover the official share of cofinancing for a number of projects simultaneously, assessing projects once they are terminated rather than in advance or assessing the entire programme of an individual NGO rather than each one of its projects. Rare until a few years ago, block grants are now used by more than one third of DAC Members, representing for some a significant share of total support for NGOs.

Table IV-3

BLOCK GRANTS AS A PERCENTAGE OF TOTAL COFINANCING IN RECENT YEARS

Canada	50 per cent in 1985 (as against 20 per cent in 1982)
CEC	Regulations limiting block grants to 20 per cent of CEC cofinancing are now being revised to raise the ceiling
Germany	New regulations allowing block grants for small micro-projects funded by the churches were established in 1984
Netherlands	82 per cent in 1982
United Kingdom	71 per cent in 1982

Countries which extend the bulk of cofinancing in the form of block grants generally also concentrate their support on a small number of experienced and trusted NGOs or upon umbrella organisations.

Umbrella organisations and other streamlining arrangements

The Netherlands extends subsidies to four major umbrella organisations (CEBEMO, ICCO, HIVOS and NOVIB) which group Dutch NGOs according to their religious and ethical connotations, e.g., Catholic, Protestant, humanistic. The system operates under arrangements which have been in existence for twenty years, with periodic adjustments to allow for greater flexibility. Under the current Joint Financing Programme, the umbrella organisations, themselves fully financed by the public sector, act as financial intermediaries on behalf of their member organisations. They are free to decide their project policy for themselves within certain limits. Projects do not have to be approved by the aid authorities nor is there a minimum share of costs that they should bear. Accountability takes the form of an annual report submitted retrospectively to the Minister for Development Co-operation. In addition, the Minister may obtain information about and exercise control over the programme by means of inspections and through "programme evaluations" (Chapter V). In Sweden, SIDA has entered into long-term co-operation agreements with 14 major NGOs, which are granted a high degree of autonomy as regards projects financed under these agreements. In 1985 they received 85 per cent of SIDA's cofinancing funds. Following new rules recently approved by SIDA, emphasis is changing from scrutiny of each application to follow-up and evaluation of implemented projects. Block grants in the United Kingdom, which account for approximately 75 per cent of total official contributions, are allocated to four major NGOs, with the remaining 25 per cent in "accountable grants" for other NGOs. In 1985 Switzerland extended 76 per cent of its official cofinancing to nine NGOs. Denmark does not extend block grants but allocates the bulk of its support for project cofinancing to two major NGOs, Danchurchaid and the Danish Red Cross. Germany has only recently introduced the possibility of block-grant funding for small projects of the churches, within the framework of new guidelines which increase the responsibility and flexibility of church agencies and reduce the administrative load of the official sector.

The adoption of block grants facilitates forward planning and continuity in NGO programmes. Some DAC Members, however, continue to rely on matching grants for individual projects and have no provision for allocating block grants, for example Belgium, Finland, Italy and the United States.

Multi-year funding

DAC Members have also sought to improve the matching-grant system by offering support over more than one year, responding to the requirements of support for partner groups in developing countries. As illustrated by a few examples below, various forms of multi-year frameworks and flexible funding are currently provided by some DAC countries and others are under consideration.

One example is the cofinancing of "renewable programmes" practised by Canada and Italy. These programmes are planned for a three-year period and provide for automatic and timely renewal if evaluation results are satisfactory. The programme "Solidarité Canada-Sahel" in particular, has some unique features including a moral commitment by CIDA towards support for local NGOs over a period of twenty years with financial commitments for five years.

Another technique known as "flexible funding" has been extended by Switzerland. Funds are made available to the NGO in advance and are not earmarked for specific activities. Professional external audits covering the totality of the NGO's income and expenditures may replace traditional financial reports on expenditure of donor funds. The idea is to provide timely financial assistance for self-help activities which have their own time requirements. This aid (so far extended only exceptionally) represents a credit line, available on the spot as and when external funds are needed.

The Netherlands has applied since 1980 a "programmatic approach" which enables the government to make a moral commitment for at least ten years to work towards the institutional strengthening of local NGOs. The system is flexible in the sense that financial commitments for three years are made on the basis of rough outlines of programmes and not for well defined and preset activities.

Belgium and the United States may extend commitments up to five years. In the case of the United States these are "partnership grants" for PVOs with a significant record of development work. Norway has signed frame agreements with some NGOs supporting operations over two or three years and may finance NGO programmes for up to ten years. Finland and Switzerland have recently adopted a three-year framework. Sweden makes an annual commitment with indicative amounts for the following two years in order to facilitate long-term planning. The European Commission currently finances projects for up to three years. It envisages offering the incentive of a longer period of support in order to encourage NGOs to adopt a more definite institution-building approach with respect to partner groups in developing countries.

Administrative costs

NGOs are allocated a certain percentage of the total amount of the cofinanced project to cover administrative costs. This percentage varies between 5 per cent in Belgium and the United Kingdom, 7 per cent in the Netherlands (the percentage may be lower for large-scale projects), 8 per cent in Switzerland, and 15 per cent or over in Italy.

Funding for feasibility studies and evaluations

Greater flexibility in support from the official sector for the funding of feasibility studies, market research, monitoring and evaluation of projects, may in a number of cases help to enhance the effectiveness of NGOs and their partners in developing countries.

A few DAC Members finance feasibility studies or pre-appraisal missions from official funds independently from the funding of the actual project (Belgium, France, Germany, Norway, Sweden, the United Kingdom and the CEC). In Norway, for instance, NORAD may bear up to 100 per cent of the costs of pre-investment studies for NGO projects. In other countries, initial studies continue to be eligible for reimbursement by the official aid agencies only as part of contributions allocated to an approved project. This is a serious procedural obstacle. It contributes to the dearth of adequate feasibility studies, whose importance in certain categories of income-generating projects cannot be overemphasized.

Many NGOs' capacity for self-evaluation is weak, which makes it difficult to adjust and improve on-going projects. Some countries, such as Switzerland, have expressed a willingness to finance joint evaluations. Norway already fully finances costs met by NGOs for evaluations. The major 1985 evaluation conducted by COTA for the CEC, mentioned in Chapter V, recommends measures and funding for strengthening evaluation departments of large NGOs and establishing joint evaluation services for smaller ones. The latter option was also considered by the research team from various French NGOs referred to in Chapter III. Some of the larger NGOs such as Misereor, on the other hand, conduct their own evaluations when they or their partners feel this is required.

Sub-contracts

Governments may also contract NGOs to serve as executing agents for official aid activities to channel food aid or emergency aid or to carry out projects of the official aid agencies. Under these contracts, project costs are fully borne by the public sector. Until a few years ago the United States was the only country contracting NGOs; but subsequently this practice has been adopted by other governments. Canada in its "country focus" approach encourages NGOs to participate in the implementation of CIDA-supported projects in main partner countries with full financing from the Canadian agency. Co-operation between CIDA and NGOs has evolved to the stage that in the Sahel region NGOs are involved as partners in the conceptualisation and design of projects, not only their implementation. The same applies to Italy's sub-contracting of NGOs, which in 1987 accounted for 41 per cent of a total allocation of 110 billion Italian lira for NGOs. In Switzerland, disbursements for sub-contracts with NGOs exceeded in 1984 the funds available for cofinancing and represented over 6 per cent of net ODA disbursements. "Intercoopération" was founded in 1982 by seven of the major Swiss NGOs with the primary purpose of implementing development projects on behalf of the Swiss government.

Contracting differs from cofinancing basically because cofinancing represents official support for activities designed by NGOs themselves. Contracting is used by governments for activities where they believe NGOs have a comparative advantage and relevant experience. An illustration is the contracting of PVOs such as Meals for Millions/Freedom from Hunger, Save the Children, Catholic Relief Services, Foster Parent Plan and others involved by US AID alongside research institutions and intergovernmental organisations in its major "Child Survival" health and nutrition programme.

Sub-contracting obviously requires the specification of the rights and obligations of all the parties involved. An important one on the NGOs' side would be that they apply to the extent feasible their principles and experience with respect to the participation of intended beneficiary groups in project planning and implementation. NGOs are eligible as implementation agencies for activities funded by the Commission of the European Communities under the Lomé III Convention, whose emphasis on rural development and food security for associated developing countries requires a major extension of actions in favour of the rural sector and small farmers. Within the framework of host-country governments' major goals and programmes, and with their agreement and that of the Commission, contracts may be awarded to NGOs for new grass-roots actions, or continuation of existing schemes.

Financial support for NGOs of developing countries

Better adjustment of cofinancing practices more specifically geared to the strengthening of indigenous NGO capacity is being sought and tried out by several aid agencies. Related procedures include direct funding of indigenous NGOs from some aid agency headquarters and various arrangements in the field. In some cases they also include the financing of indigenous NGOs' overhead costs, the use of revolving funds and the provision of credit and loan guarantees.

Funding of host-country NGOs

Up to the late 1970s, support for host-country NGOs was, as a rule, only extended indirectly through aid-agency collaboration with Member-country NGOs. Most Member countries also have a long tradition of funds at the disposal of diplomatic missions for use at their discretion for charitable or other purposes, but these are usually very modest amounts. Canada was a forerunner in establishing a decade ago a division within CIDA for international NGOs to support their affiliates in developing countries. Since then, more and more DAC countries have introduced various programmes for the provision of official financial support to NGOs of developing countries, notably Canada, Denmark, France, Norway, Sweden, Switzerland and the United States.

Major current programmes may be categorised as follows:

-- Direct aid to indigenous organisations in developing countries from aid agency headquarters as a normal feature of co-operation with NGOs (currently mainly Norway and to a lesser extent Switzerland); or through special programmes (Canada's "Africa 2000" programme); or institutions specially created by the public sector (the Inter-American Development Foundation and the African Development Foundation established by Congress in the United States);

-- The establishment of funds at aid missions, accessible to host-country NGOs and other NGOs -- mainly the United States with its substantial "umbrella grants"; Canada (some $Can 27 million in 1987 in 115 countries) and, as of 1985, Sweden, with SIDA extending funds managed by embassies for local NGOs' projects complementary to bilateral programmes; Norway is now also adding local-mission administered funds for in-country organisations;

-- Special funds at embassies to support local initiatives for women (the Netherlands, Norway and Sweden);

-- Funds at the disposal of aid missions for the financing of local "micro-projects" [mainly the CEC and France (French disbursements in 1986 under this heading amounted to $4.3 million)].

Direct aid from aid agency headquarters

Selected illustrations are provided hereafter. In recent years, Norway surveyed local NGOs in its main partner countries, with the purpose of allocating a larger share of aid directly to indigenous NGOs. In 1984, NORAD's direct contributions to national NGOs of developing countries already amounted to 15 per cent of total official allocations to voluntary agencies. Norwegian aid for host-country NGOs is now also branching out to include the allocation of funds to NORAD missions in certain developing countries.

Support from Switzerland for strengthening farmers' organisations in West Africa in the form of flexible funding for the international "Six S" association has been mentioned already. Flexible funding in this case and in the case of CESAO, however, is linked with the registration of these non-profit organisations under Swiss law. A more modest example of direct aid relates to a two-year agreement in 1984 with the Xaviers' Institute of Social Services in Ranchi, India, whereby XISS in turn provided loans to small rural initiatives in a district of Bihar using grant aid for establishing a revolving loan fund.

In-country "umbrella grants" of the United States

The United States may provide financial support to host-country NGOs through their field missions. For this purpose US AID uses "umbrella grants" whereby country missions are allocated funds ranging from $250 000 up to approximately $5 million annually for use by US PVOs as well as host-country NGOs. Country missions are responsible for deciding on the size of these funds, the selection of programmes and their duration. The umbrella approach started in Indonesia in 1971, initially funding US voluntary agencies. Many missions in Asia followed suit, and in the early 1980s several missions in African and Latin American countries have also set up umbrella grants (in Jamaica, Kenya, Senegal, Somalia and Zaire among others), and various others are designing or considering similar mechanisms. [A lively account of the emergence of domestic Caribbean NGOs following repeated injections of PVO funds and experience is provided by Terry Lacey in the "dossier" on development NGOs in The Courier No. 104, July-August 1987, CEC, Brussels.] Models established by the various missions vary considerably and the procedures adopted may facilitate access to funding by local NGOs (PVO funding procedures are generally quite complex and sophisticated). In some developing countries, AID missions have taken measures to ensure access by local NGOs, by earmarking a share of the umbrella fund for smaller grants or by other means. Through consultative services for guidance and management training, a second phase of the umbrella fund in Indonesia helped an increasing number of Indonesian voluntary agencies to receive support. The aid mission in Zaire contracted a PVO to implement components of a programme through both local and US agencies.

Examples of US AID support for strengthening host-country intermediary institutions include a $3 million grant in 1983 to the Jamaica Council of Voluntary Social Services to build up the capacity of such services; an $8 million grant to MIDAS (Micro-Industries Development and Assistance Society), a local non-profit agency in Bangladesh, to help its small business development activities up to 1992; and a $1 million grant linking the US PVO consortium PACT (Private Agencies Collaborating Together) with an umbrella organisation in Guatemala, ASINDES, to strengthen its affiliates and their productive and social activities.

In the Philippines, the programme began in 1980, providing small grants to voluntary agencies involved in rural and urban development work. Programmes currently supported in the province of Negros Occidental are conducted by US PVOs and a host of local associations. The fall in sugar prices dramatically extended unemployment and misery in this area of over 2 million people, where four out of five sugar-worker households are estimated to be below subsistence-level income. The programme recognises that its activities are not a substitute for structural reform but aims at meeting immediate basic needs including food, and at reducing dependence on sugar over the short and medium term, mainly by supporting food production. In 1986, CARE and Save the Children were thus involved in Negros Occidental alongside Filipino non-profit groups and local organisations in health and nutrition programmes, productive activities, land settlement programmes, the retrieving of land from former sugar plantations, vocational training and micro-enterprise development.

Other DAC Members' in-country NGO funding

As noted above, Norway is also devoting a fraction of its fast-growing allocations for NGOs to in-country funding through its missions in the main partner countries. Flexibility has now been enhanced by a policy to let the NORAD missions manage an annual allocation. For 1986 this amount was globally approximately $10 million. The NORAD mission is authorised to support modestly sized projects up to a ceiling of $34 000 each. Decisions regarding larger support must be made by NORAD/Oslo. In-country organisations are eligible for support under the same conditions as Norwegian NGOs. The main sectors involved in recent years have been education, health, agriculture/forestry, including environmental protection and water supplies. Larger country recipients until now have been Bangladesh (2), Sri Lanka, Kenya (3) and India. Allocations to in-country organisations amounted to 2.4 per cent of NORAD's total NGO budget in 1982 and to 17 per cent in 1986.

Switzerland allows for allocations by its in-country DDA co-ordination bureaux, in developing countries where it has established such bureaux, of between $10 000 and $50 000 per NGO per year. (In other developing countries, Swiss missions have available funds of $25 000 each which they may use for small projects of local NGOs.)

Limitations

Bilateral funding of host-country NGOs by official aid agencies was still small in 1983, when it stood at $37 million (with the United States accounting for over 80 per cent of this amount) but it has been expanding considerably since then. Some DAC Members such as Belgium and the United Kingdom still have regulations precluding direct financing of NGOs of other nationalities.

For a number of reasons, there is no consensus among official aid agencies and NGOs on the desirability of such bilateral funding. Some believe that support for host-country organisations is best channelled through DAC Members' NGOs. This remains in any event the way most of it is provided in practice.

Revolving funds and credit

DAC Members provide contributions to NGOs in grant form. Some of them, notably Germany, Switzerland and the United States allow for such grants to be used by the implementing NGO for extending loans whose reimbursements in local currency can be used for new loans (revolving funds).

France introduced in 1985 a special credit scheme to support productive grass-roots initiatives. Under this scheme, loans are extended by the Caisse centrale de coopération économique (CCCE), an official financial institution, to viable small productive activities promoted by individuals or groups with visible support from their communities. Interest rates are between 0 and 5 per cent, with a maturity of three to seven years. These credits may be associated with complementary financing such as grants provided by NGOs. A total of $1.3 million has been allocated for an initial experimental stage of this scheme with a ceiling of $50 000 for any single project.

Another option for donors is illustrated by the experience of Switzerland and, earlier, the CEC, contributing to the Inter-American Development Bank for its "Programme for the Financing of Small Projects". The programme operates through a two-step approach: IDB extends loans of up to $0.5 million to intermediary organisations, which are non-profit institutions such as co-operatives, foundations or producers' associations, as well as public-sector development institutions. Intermediaries in turn lend amounts of commonly up to $1 000 to low-income individuals or groups with no access to bank loans. Loans to intermediaries may be for up to forty years, with a ten-year grace period and a fee of 1 per cent. They fund revolving funds to which the intermediaries have in some instances been able to attract additional resources. Loans may be supplemented by non-reimbursable grants for technical co-operation and support. Between 1978 and 1986, cumulative IDB loans for such small projects totalled $63.8 million.

2. THE UNITED NATIONS SYSTEM

Consultative status

Between the two world wars, NGOs focused much of their effort and attention on the activities of intergovernmental organisations in areas that concerned them. The international labour movement was central to the creation of the International Labour Organisation (ILO), with its tripartite system of representation for governments, labour and business. Neither the League of Nations nor the ILO established formal consultative or participatory status for NGOs, but in the various committees of the League they were allowed to speak, present reports, initiate discussions, propose resolutions and amendments, and be assigned to sub-committees.

Pressures from representatives of such non-profit groups as the Carnegie Endowment for International Peace led the 1945 San Francisco Conference to adopt Article 71 of the United Nations Charter. This limits NGOs, however, to interventions on economic and social issues. This was less than the statutory consultation on political questions which NGOs had aimed for, but it was unprecedented in establishing formal relations between "interest groups" and an intergovernmental body. The tensions at the time of the drafting of the Charter have continued up to now, as NGOs apply pressure nationally and internationally on issues which have substantial political aspects, such as disarmament, human rights and women's rights. Article 71 of the Charter limited consultation with NGOs to ECOSOC. NGOs were divided into three categories according to their interest in ECOSOC work: Categories I, II and Roster. Category I grants privileges such as attending meetings of ECOSOC and, most significantly, to propose agenda items for consideration by ECOSOC and its subsidiary bodies. Category II NGOs are those whose competence lies only in a few of the "fields of activity" covered by ECOSOC: they have all the privileges of Category I except the right to propose agenda items. Roster

NGOs are those that ECOSOC or the Secretary-General consider "can make occasional and useful contributions to the work of the Council".

In the specialised agencies, relationships with NGOs are usually specified in the constitution of the organisation and either follow the ECOSOC pattern or make no distinction between categories of NGOs (4).

NGOs' support for UN agencies

Special NGOs to support the United Nations or some of the specialised agencies were created in earlier decades in a great number of DAC countries. The United Nations associations, for instance, still play a major role in several Nordic countries in development education. Whether their legal status makes them NGOs or quasi-NGOs, bodies such as national UNICEF committees and committees on refugees play an important role in fostering within DAC countries humanitarian causes which are institutionally dealt with by UN bodies. In some cases these bodies also act as fund-raisers, e.g. for UNICEF.

UN agencies' support for NGOs

The role which FAO's Freedom from Hunger/Action for Development played in the early 1960s in promoting national associations and campaigns was mentioned previously. It currently maintains a promotional role in holding consultations between donor sources and developing-country NGOs. Freedom from Hunger associations have been created in a number of developing countries and some are particularly active, e.g., in Kenya, with support mainly from the German counterpart, Deutsche Welthungerhilfe, and more recently the Australian Freedom from Hunger and Italy's Terra Nuova. Another example of co-operation was the formation in the 1970s of COPAC (Committee for the Promotion of Aid to Co-operatives), representing the joint interests in co-operative development of the UN, FAO, ILO, the International Co-operative Alliance, International Federation of Agricultural Producers, International Federation of Plantation, Agricultural and Allied Workers and the World Council of Credit Unions. In 1988-89, COPAC will examine the findings of a series of evaluations conducted by UNDP, ILO, the British ODA, US AID, ACORD and other agencies concerning these agencies' assistance to co-operative development.

Contracting NGOs for project implementation

Contracting is done in particular by the Office of the UN High Commissioner for Refugees, UNFPA (the UN Fund for Population Assistance), and the World Bank. An illustration in the case of UNHCR may be provided by the experience of the Lutheran World Service in conjunction with the national council of churches of Tanzania in resettling thousands of refugees from Burundi and Rwanda, enabling them to lead a productive life and contributing to the development of the country which granted them asylum. UNFPA has worked closely with NGOs since its inception in 1969. Indeed, many NGOs were active in the field of population long before UNFPA was established, often paving the way in areas that governments deemed too sensitive. For the period 1969-86, about 10 per cent of UNFPA's budget was spent on activities implemented by NGOs in 796 projects, that is, a cumulative $145.2 million. (A separate section deals with the World Bank's practice.)

Co-operation in the field and in DAC countries

UNICEF is among the best-known UN agencies in co-operation in the field, joining forces, through its cadre of experienced in-country staff, with NGOs as well as other official agencies in a variety of activities, especially at the grass-roots level in rural areas and in deprived urban settings. Within UNICEF's concept of the "Grand Alliance for Children" a large number of NGOs co-operate with UNICEF on a wide variety of activities, for instance, Defence for Children International on global advocacy activities, the Lutheran World Federation on hand-pump maintenance in Zimbabwe and village and community Rotary Clubs on the global immunisation campaign. UNICEF has also played a leading role in documenting the impact on the poor of structural adjustment programmes and facilitating the dialogue between NGOs and the World Bank on this problem.

Within DAC countries, close co-operation has evolved over the years between European NGOs and the UN-non-governmental Liaison Service (UN-NGLS) in Geneva, responsible for liaison with developmental NGOs in Europe. UN-NGLS has a record of working effectively through national and international consultations, particularly on development education. A similar service in New York, in charge of liaison with NGOs in the Western Hemisphere, has been active in assisting the information-sharing and networking functions of NGOs in Africa in the tree-planting or "social forestry" sector, and helps the sharing of documentation on agro-forestry in the Sahel region. It also promotes a development education project with focus on Africa in Canada and the United States.

Specially relevant to NGOs' productive and skill-training projects is the support provided by the ILO's rural vocational training and income-earning activities, which assist the development of artisans' groups and women's groups in various developing countries. The ILO seeks to extend its co-operation with NGOs in these activities. A survey contributed by NORAD to the ILO to identify initial action and areas for co-operation with NGOs in rural skills-training in several countries of East Africa was mentioned in Chapter II.

Establishment of cofinancing by UNDP and IFAD

A senior adviser on grass-roots and NGO matters was first appointed in UNDP in 1984, following two brain-storming sessions conducted for UNDP staff with the participation of the Society for International Development (SID). In January 1987, an NGO Division with an initial allocation of $1 million was established at UNDP's headquarters in New York. By 1988, the opportunity of UNDP collaboration was offered in 40 countries. Main features are as follows. Participating countries will be rotated from year to year. Funding for the programme is assured at the level of $1 million annually through 1991. NGO requests for funding must be addressed to UNDP Resident Representatives. Northern NGOs are not entirely excluded but strong preference will be given to indigenous NGOs. One of the longer-term aims is to sensitise UNDP structures to the potential for co-operating with NGOs.

Following discussions between NGOs and the International Fund for Agricultural Development (IFAD), initiated by an ICVA/IFAD meeting in November 1986, IFAD developed in 1987 an IFAD/NGO Extended Co-operation

Programme to finance NGO pilot activities from IFAD's regular resources and voluntary contributions. Pilot activities should be relevant to IFAD activities, such as testing new technologies presenting advantages for the poorest people, testing new institutional approaches, and training programmes aimed at improving organisation systems such as farmers' groups. Initial IFAD resources earmarked for this programme amount to $350 000 annually.

3. THE WORLD BANK

General

World Bank relations with NGOs are mainly of two kinds: contracting NGOs for the implementation of project components where they appear to have a comparative advantage over other categories of implementors, subject to the proviso that a request is needed from the host government; and consultations. Recent policy statements and organisational changes appear to attribute higher priority to research into strategies on poverty issues and related consultations with NGOs.

Increased collaboration will require continuing promotional efforts. The tripartite sector workshops which the Bank convenes from time to time for joint consultation to consider issues in given sectors and regions are the leading promotional instrument developed so far. In Sub-Saharan Africa, it has been used most extensively by the Bank's Population/Health/Nutrition Department, but also in the education sector, and, more recently, in forestry, rural water supply and fisheries sectors. Bank staff interested in promoting greater collaboration with NGOs are also pushing for more systematic canvassing of collaboration possibilities, in selected sectors, as part of the Bank's routine project identification and project preparation procedures.

Illustrations from experience in Sub-Saharan Africa

For the DAC seminar held in June 1986, the World Bank contributed a report specially prepared by Mr. George Baldwin, consultant, on its co-operation with NGOs in agricultural and rural development in Sub-Saharan Africa. The report estimates that formal collaboration existed in about 5 per cent of the 550 Bank-assisted projects (all sectors) implemented in the region in 1986. It provides a selection of examples of formal and informal co-operation in agriculture and rural development projects and other activities, and presents four summary case studies. It is summarised hereafter in some detail as it provides rare insights on relevant experience.

In agriculture, the Swaziland Rural Development Project implemented in 1977-83 and evaluated in 1985 identified weaknesses which in the opinion of the consultant strengthen the case for increasing co-operation with NGOs. There was inadequate communication on local needs, aspirations and plans. The basic institutional goal of drawing together different aspects of rural development under the management of a single unit at both village and central government level could not be achieved. Another failed experience relates to the Geita District Cotton Expansion Project in Tanzania. The Geita District had been selected because of favourable physical and social factors, including a strong co-operative movement (110 primary societies, four ginneries, two oil mills, a transport fleet, a co-operative union supplying farm inputs and credit, handling the purchase, transport and ginning of cotton, and purchasing and milling maize and paddy). Shortly after the project became effective, however, the government collectivised the area and abolished all the co-operatives, transferring their functions to parastatal organisations. A different kind of problem was met in an attempt to work through co-operatives for crop and livestock development in a region of Gambia. Weaknesses of the co-operatives were not identified in time and widespread fraud faulted the arrangements for credit. The Bank and ILO are now engaged in strengthening the co-operatives. In Zaire the lack of government institutions in many rural areas is to some extent compensated by NGO services, especially church-linked, in education, health and agriculture. Offices for development set up in Catholic dioceses, for example, provide a wide variety of economic and social services, and complement with their own profit-making projects the help received from external NGOs. A measure of the success of NGOs is provided by the Shaba province, where two NGOs obtain full cost recovery on the physical inputs they provide to farmers, and also charge farmers the full cost for the extension services. There are no prospects for establishing governmental services in the area for some years to come and the approach proposed to support agricultural development is to pass IDA and IFAD funds through the government to these agencies, which will be expected to repay the government part of the funds.

In activities in rural areas in sectors other than agriculture, the Bank has co-operated with CARE in primary school construction in Liberia and rural road construction and maintenance in Sierra Leone. The most extensive collaboration so far between the Bank, NGOs and a government has occurred in a population project in Kenya. In a note prepared for the Bank's Water Supply and Urban Department, it was estimated that NGOs currently contribute around $180 million annually to rural water supplies, about three times the expenditures of UNICEF (the leading UN agency in this field) and three times annual Bank loans. In 1983 the Bank, with Oxfam help, organised a meeting with NGOs to ask for their co-operation in its pump-testing programmes, but the NGO representatives present declined the offer, because they had an unfavourable image of the Bank.

The summary case studies highlight in the first place the tripartite sector workshops sponsored by the Bank to discuss sector problems with NGOs and host-country governments. Between 1983 and 1986, eight such workshops were held, two on education in East Africa, four on health and population (in Botswana, Gambia, Kenya and Rwanda), one on water and sanitation in Abidjan and one on forestry in Kenya.

A second case reviewed related to a 1985 grant of $0.5 million provided by the Bank in Togo to set up a co-ordinating NGO mechanism and a revolving fund for small grants, under the guidance of a tripartite steering committee including government, NGOs and the Bank. This experience has met with difficulties because of its top-down and government-led approach.

A third case relates to a $5.1 million project for the construction of three major and 18 satellite primary health care centres in north-western Mali using a construction technique developed by an IRED-related NGO based in Burkina Faso, ADAUA (Association pour le développement d'une architecture naturelle et d'un urbanisme africains). ADAUA has developed bricks made of stabilised soil, with strict quality control, innovative architectural design derived from traditional forms, resulting in low-cost, import-saving, labour-intensive construction. ADAUA found it difficult at first to manage such a large project. These difficulties were overcome, however, and the staff required was recruited in West Africa for the Bamako headquarters and to supervise contruction. Mali is saving one third of the cost of conventional construction costs and more than 50 per cent of the normal foreign exchange costs. Teams of masons, brickmakers and labourers are given training, in subjects which include accounting, estimating and procurement, with the expectation that some of them will be able to operate as small contractors when the project ends.

A fourth case relates to informal collaboration between the project officers of a Bank-financed project and an NGO project, each of which was having its own difficulties in the Baringo semi-arid area of Kenya. Rough comparisons showed that in the NGO project activities such as extension, seed production and maintenance were being made at 10-15 per cent of the cost in the official project, with qualitatively superior methods in extension work.

The World Bank report also suggests that official projects might gain in effectiveness by prior study of technologies adopted in NGO projects in the same area: the example given is the "water harvesting" method developed by Oxfam in the Yatenga region of Burkina Faso, whereby rain water is arrested by low, crescent-shaped lines of stone along the contours of the land. The water can then seep into the soil allowing trees and crops to be grown.

The NGO/World Bank Committee

A consultative NGO/World Bank Committee was established in 1982. It comprises on a rotating five-year basis NGOs of both developed and developing countries, including, for the latter, BRAC of Bangladesh, Kenya's Women's Financial Trust and the Zimbabwe Freedom from Hunger Campaign. In order to have a central base from which to maintain their dialogue with the World Bank, NGOs forming part of this committee have recently become an ad hoc working group of ICVA.

The NGO/World Bank Committee's discussions currently focus on major issues such as debt and the impact of structural adjustment programmes on low-income populations. The sixth meeting of the Committee, held in November 1986, was the first to be addressed by the President of the Bank, who assured NGOs of the Bank's intention to seek their input into Bank policy and project formulation. At first the dialogue on the debt issue appears to have been difficult. NGOs of the NGO/World Bank Committee were invited to contribute to the Bank's drafting of a paper on adjustment and poverty for the April 1987 World Bank/IMF Development Committee meeting, but few of the comments of the NGO group were reflected in the paper. Subsequently, the 20 major NGOs in the group argued in a collective letter to the President of the Bank that its plans for handling the debt crisis should be substantially modified to protect the poor from the pressures of adjustment in the world recession [ICVA News, Nos. 121-124, 1987.] Given the crucial importance attributed by both sides to these issues, the dialogue is being maintained, notwithstanding its difficulties. In 1987, Bank exchanges with church groups focussed on debt, adjustment policies and the need to protect the poor. Highlights were discussions with the Catholic Church on its statement on international debt, and participation in conferences organised in Mexico and Washington by Lutheran and Quaker groups, by Interfaith Action for Economic Justice (a public policy coalition of US religious groups) and a meeting on debt and poverty organised by French Catholic and Protestant NGOs. The Bank also helped finance a workshop in Oxford on debt, adjustment and the needs of the poor, which was a major opportunity for NGO representatives to discuss their analysis of these issues among themselves and with representatives of the UN system. This workshop, held in September 1987, also contributed to the networking of NGOs across national frontiers in the public opinion campaigns on debt and the poorest countries, which they waged in Europe and North America in 1988. (A report on this workshop was issued by UN-NGLS: see reference in Ch. VI.) Some "compensatory programmes" to alleviate hardship have been set up, at times in collaboration with NGOs or following an initiative taken by them. For example, the Bank is supporting the start-up phase of an Emergency Social Fund (ESF) of the Bolivian government for unemployed miners and other poor people most seriously hit by the economic turmoil which preceded and accompanied recent adjustment measures. Initial experimentation, which led to the establishment of ESF, was carried out by Oxfam. An initiative called "Programme of Actions to Mitigate the Social Costs of Adjustment" (PAMSCAD) in Ghana was launched with a pledging conference convened by the government of Ghana and the World Bank in Geneva in February 1988, with the participation of several donor governments, multilateral agencies and donor and Ghanaian NGOs. About one-half of the over $80 million requested for this programme was pledged directly at the conference. As can be seen, over the past 2-3 years relations have intensified, seeking increased NGO involvement in World Bank operations and more effective policy dialogue on selected development issues. This is reflected in the Consensus Conclusions of the World Bank/NGO Committee meeting of November 1987 in Santo Domingo which concisely map out orientations for collaboration (these conclusions were published in the ICVA News issue of December 1987).

Organisational up-grading

The World Bank's reorganisation announced on 4th May 1987 situated future work of the NGO/World Bank Committeee in the new Strategic Planning and Review Department, under a senior vice-president for policy, planning and research.

4. REGIONAL DEVELOPMENT BANKS

In July 1987, the Board of Directors of the Asian Development Bank approved a policy paper aimed at enabling the Bank to co-operate with NGOs, its main objectives being increased effectiveness in assistance for poor and disadvantaged groups and better support for environmental protection in the AsDB's developing member countries. Co-operation can take the form of seeking information from NGOs in project preparation and design, the recruitment of NGOs as consultants, contractors and implementing agencies, or cofinancing, subject to the prior agreement of the host-country governments concerned. This decision made AsDB the first regional development bank to develop an explicit policy of co-operation with NGOs. ⌈See Asian Development Bank, The

Bank's Co-operation with Non-governmental Organisations, June 1987. An information booklet on the AsDB's co-operation with NGOs is announced.]

NOTES AND REFERENCES

1. An overview of the co-operation with NGOs is published yearly by the German Ministry for Economic Co-operation. For 1986, see Entwicklungs-Politik, Materialen No 73, September 1987.

2. Bangladesh: Country Study and Norwegian Aid Review, the Christian Michelsen Institute, Bergen, 1986.

3. A. Tostensen and J. Scott (eds.), Kenya: Country Study and Norwegian Aid Review, the Christian Michelsen Institute, Bergen, 1987.

4. Kilgore and C. Roosevelt, op. cit. (see notes to Chapter I).

Chapter V

A REVIEW OF EVALUATIONS AND RESEARCH

Summary review of major evaluations by country (1979-87)

In many DAC countries samples of projects cofinanced with NGOs undergo systematic evaluation by the official aid agency, sometimes with participation of NGO representatives on the evaluation team. In some others evaluation is more rarely used. Since the early 1980s, in addition to evaluating single projects, some DAC Members have launched broader assessments of NGOs' performance and of co-operative arrangements between NGOs and the official aid agencies. Were NGOs satisfactory partners? Should the official sector keep supporting them? This chapter highlights findings from several recent evaluations. Three evaluations, in particular, go beyond the specific concerns of the individual aid agency which commissioned them and are presented in somewhat greater detail. One is Judith Tendler's evaluation of 1982, which was a first and seminal clarification of concepts for assessing NGOs' actual roles against their own declared goals. The second is a major exercise conducted in 1985 by the Commission of European Communities. Reasons for signalling it include its wide coverage of NGO projects from various European countries and its suggestions for practical improvements to enhance achievement of NGOs' goals. Finally, a recent Dutch report on rural development projects in Burkina Faso and Mali illustrates some of the very difficult circumstances in which NGOs intervene. It forms part of the new evaluation system introduced in 1980 within a highly decentralised framework for co-operation between the Dutch government and NGOs. (See the sections in this chapter on the CEC, the Netherlands and the United States.)

Over the past five years, most DAC Members have evaluated NGO projects and several have also evaluated their own arrangements and programmes for the cofinancing of NGO programmes. Several other Members have evaluation studies underway that will enable them to assess the validity of their rationale for co-operating with NGOs. Based on evaluations already published (whose major findings are briefly summarised below) some tentative conclusions can be drawn, keeping in mind that the evaluation of NGO activities should be viewed in the context of the long-term efforts for institution-building and for changing attitudes and capabilities and not only as quantitative achievements in the short term. Success of NGO operations depends on a complex set of factors including macroeconomic and socio-political "environmental variables" beyond NGOs' control. The institution-building goals of NGOs may typically take ten years or more for meaningful and sustainable results to be assured.

Available evaluations tend to confirm the comparative advantage of NGOs in their ability to work at the grass-roots level, to address basic human needs and to operate in remote areas often unserved by national governments or official donors. Various studies, however, reveal that the NGO record is uneven, differing from country to country, from NGO to NGO and from sector to sector. Limitations, weaknesses and constraints have been identified in a number of cases, indicating that there is still scope for clarifying goals and improving effectiveness.

Canada

Canadian NGOs and CIDA see the need for a broad, rigorous evaluation of NGOs' wide range of developmental activities, particularly given the rapid growth of official funds for cofinancing, and the funds of the NGO sector itself, since the previous African famine of the early 1970s. Accordingly a major evaluation was carried out by CIDA in 1984-85 in order to assess the past performance of its NGO programme, including a large number of projects (420) jointly sponsored by CIDA and Canadian NGOs. The evaluation found that the overall success of projects in achieving their objectives was positive in terms of sustainability, multiplier effect and strengthening of local NGOs. Eighty per cent of the projects were still operating two to five years after the Canadian funding was over. About one third of all projects had attained financial autonomy. Multiplier effects observed were the spreading of project effects beyond the intended beneficiary population and an impact on government policies. Determinants of project success were mobilisation of technical and administrative resources, community participation and soundness of project design. Overall, the NGO programme showed a strong rural emphasis and a clear focus on the poor. Women were surprisingly the specified target group in only one out of five projects. Operating policies and procedures were considered appropriate but it was felt that block and multi-year funding could be used more widely. (CIDA, Corporate Evaluation of CIDA's Non-Governmental Organisations Programme, October 1986.)

Another major evaluation was undertaken by the independent North-South Institute in Ottawa, whose purpose was to test the validity of "articles of faith" held by NGOs on their own role by assessing their performance in developmental and emergency aid and, to a lesser extent, development education activities in Canada. A consultative group of NGO senior representatives guides the Institute's research team. Approximately 150 Canadian NGOs replied to a detailed questionnaire and field research was started in several developing countries in 1986 with funding from the Government of Alberta, CIDA, four foundations and eleven NGOs. The report subsequently published in English and French is one of the most thoughtful studies of NGOs. Much of it illustrates the experience of Canadian NGOs but a number of considerations are of a more general interest. Some of these -- relating to efficiency and to future prospects -- are summarised hereafter. The relations between costs and cost-effectiveness are not simple, indeed excessive concern with cost reductions may be at the cost of long-term effectiveness, in particular in activities to alleviate poverty which may be quite administrative-intensive. The most relevant standards of efficiency for NGOs are: their ability to mobilise private resources; the long-term impact of their projects as measured by: a) sustainability and, b) extent of replication; and the effectiveness of co-operation among agencies. On the ability to mobilise private resources, the report notes that these include not only donations by the Canadian public but, as well, contributions by beneficiaries (indeed the report notes that user-payments and credit may constitute tools for the financial autonomy of Southern NGOs). Sustainability appears to be a fairly weak point, linked to the weak capacity or interest of NGOs to develop income-generating activities, requiring greater emphasis on project design and careful monitoring. Replication is probably difficult to identify in studies of individual projects: studies of whole sectors would be more appropriate. However, NGOs appear to have a limited capacity for replication, and a major cause may be the poor quality and insufficient availability of information on successful projects. Closer agency co-operation and co-ordination bring a number of benefits but are not cost-less. Looking into the future, the report sees four main challenges for Canadian NGOs to develop a more strategic orientation. One is a gradual devolution of responsibility to Southern NGOs, which are best placed to make decisions and appreciate the social, political and economic context of their work. A second issue is autonomy, especially in view of the growth in official funding in "non-responsive" areas, for specific countries or types of operations (e.g. immunisations), which increasingly determines the programme agenda for NGOs. While in theory the remedy is a renewed emphasis on private fund-raising, in practice it may require a growth in official sector "responsiveness" and care on the part of NGOs to maintain an appropriate funding "mix". Ultimately, maintaining an attitude of self-questioning is seen by the report as a better guarantee of autonomy than limiting the volume of public-sector funding. The presence of field personnel is seen as encoraging attitudes of self-questioning. Increased inter-agency co-ordination would provide greater integration of project funding and domestic development education, and more involvement of Third World people in the deliberations of Canadian NGOs. Finally, also required is a style of management that is effective while allowing for participation, the sharing of information and flexibility (Tim Brodhead and Brent Herbert-Copley with Anne-Marie Lambert, Bridges of Hope? Canadian Voluntary Agencies and the Third World, The North-South Institute, Ottawa, 1988).

Commission of the European Communities

In 1981 and 1985 the Commission undertook two major evaluations of the projects it had cofinanced with NGOs from its member countries. The earlier study was based on a comparative evaluation of 26 NGO projects in five countries. In general, projects were found to be effective in improving the living standards of poor communities by helping to satisfy basic needs. Project objectives were achieved and implementation was efficient and timely. Despite generally positive findings, critical points were also raised about how the capacity of local populations for self-help efforts could be enhanced through involving beneficiaries more in project design. Also NGO activities too often duplicated host-country structures with no prospect of continuity once the external NGO withdrew. NGOs needed support to establish in-country co-ordination at local and national levels; and, in order to enhance flexibility and sustainability, organised local groups should be funded in a less pre-programmed fashion so that financial resources could be used as and when required. [CEC, Evaluation Study of 26 Cofinanced NGO Projects in Five Countries, SEC (81)1052, 1981.]

A second wide-ranging evaluation was prepared in 1985 under the responsibility of the Collectif d'échanges pour la technologie appropriée (COTA) for the Evaluation Department of the Commission's Development Directorate. The report drew on findings of 32 project evaluations in 17 different countries in Africa, Asia and Latin America. Projects were chosen for their broadly successful results, since it would be easier to identify lessons of general application from projects which were working well. In the first place, the study proposed a project assessment against four criteria: effectiveness, efficiency, viability and impact.

-- <u>Effectiveness</u> compared the actual project performance with targets formulated initially. Effectiveness was found to be generally good. The concept, however, was not applicable to several categories of projects: e.g., those promoting social consciousness as well as multipurpose and non-productive projects.

-- <u>Efficiency</u> measured tangible results against the means employed to achieve them (cost-efficiency). Even where efficiency was measurable in this sense, the analysis was generally thwarted by the failure of project management to measure the financial value of recurring inputs and, more importantly, of outputs. The report considered this failure an important finding in itself.

-- The criterion of <u>viability</u>, considered to be the most important, was defined as the capacity of the project to sustain itself after external funding ended. The picture which emerged was a mixed one, with positive and negative aspects. Several projects appeared likely to experience difficulty in securing inputs and reaching markets once project support ceased. Recipients generally seemed to have acquired the necessary technical skills to operate on a self-sufficient basis, but managerial capabilities appeared to be questionable in almost half of the cases studied.

-- <u>Impact</u> encompassed the general developmental consequences for different groups of people and institutions. Relatively few projects were started with the explicit goal of working in the interest of the poorest groups. Many showed an inadequate understanding of power relations within the project's target community. Hence, the poorest groups (and women) were often excluded from project benefits. The clearest positive impact was evident in institutional development: there were many instances where local self-help groups were formed as a result of the project, and where weak communities improved their bargaining position for provision of government services.

The analysis based on these four criteria showed that there was clearly substantial scope for project improvement. The study further identified certain common features pertaining to the more successful projects.

-- Conduct <u>preliminary investigations</u> to determine how they can intervene in response to the priority needs of intended beneficiaries. In less successful projects, in contrast, the capacity or will to conduct such enquiries was lacking.

-- Start with the <u>ends</u> and then proceed to identifying the appropriate means for attaining them. Unsuccessful organisations tend to focus on the means for improvement, especially the techniques and provision of services with which they are more familiar.

-- Possess the <u>technical knowledge</u> required to respond to needs or seek it from other agencies.

-- Develop sufficiently comprehensive approaches. Unsuccessful projects fail to do so: many irrigation projects only bring water to the fields and make no provision for improving farming practices; many training projects fail to connect with production and employment opportunities.

-- Facilitate the development of strong indigenous institutions. This is done, inter alia, by transferring management functions to the local group at an early stage in project operations, and by helping group members gain access to credit through revolving funds or bank loans rather than relying throughout on grant aid.

A final general point, reflecting a weakness found in nearly all the projects investigated, concerned the capacity and inclination of organisations to monitor and evaluate their own progress or to see these exercises as tools for internal management. In an overwhelming majority of cases, monitoring and evaluation tended to be seen as chores whose only function was to satisfy the requirements of funding agencies.

The report's two major recommendations aim principally at enhancing the development of viable local institutions. Over the short term, urgent steps should be taken to improve methods of project identification and appraisal and subsequent project monitoring and evaluation. This would require more thorough preparatory work with a sharper identification of intended beneficiaries and routine ex ante specification of likely benefits for the poorer people, women and ethnic and other deprived minorities; proper consultation with, and involvement of, beneficiaries in project planning; clarification of objectives; more thorough financial analysis, including expected recurrent costs; establishment of secure input lines and market outlets; provision for project replication. Over the longer term, the funding agency's procedures should be revised to allow for greater project flexibility in implementation, and to extend the block-grant system to a larger number of cofinanced operations. [G. de Crombrugghe, M. Howes and M. Nieuwerk, An Evaluation of CEC Small Development Projects, CEC VIII/435/86-EN, 1985.]

France

In France, the services for co-operation and development of the Ministry of Foreign Affairs conducted in 1983 an evaluation of rural development activities of the NGO Frères des hommes in Burkina Faso. The main conclusions were that the projects had unintentionally favoured the better-off farmers mainly because of high input costs. Project cost-effectiveness compared favourably with a similar programme run by host-country services, but improvements in farming techniques which the projects sought to introduce did not spread as widely as had been expected. [J.L. Amselle and E. Grégoire, Actions Frères des hommes dans l'est de la Haute Volta, Ministry of Foreign Affairs, Paris, 1983.]

An economic analysis of 30 NGO projects in trade, banking and agriculture in Senegal and Burkina Faso was conducted in 1984 by the French researcher Marie-Christine Guéneau. Sixty per cent of them had created additional income. Small projects had a positive impact on seasonal employment during the dry season. Most projects had innovative features. But only about one fourth were able to continue once external assistance ended. NGOs tended not to co-operate with one another nor with existing host-country services and this had negative consequences on farmers once foreign assistance was terminated. NGOs had a positive impact on local cohesion and village-level organisations, especially farmers' organisations and cereal banks. The study also found that the operating costs of projects carried out by expatriate NGOs were higher than those of projects implemented by local NGOs because of much higher salaries paid to expatriate staff. Finally, it appeared that one of the main shortcomings in a number of projects was the inadequacy of leadership training particularly in accounting and management. [M-C. Guéneau, Afrique : les petits projets de développement sont-ils efficaces ? Editions Harmattan, Paris, 1986.]

Germany

Case studies conducted on over 30 initiatives and institutions in developing countries relevant to self-help by the special unit of the Federal Ministry for Economic Co-operation "ES 31" are mentioned in Chapter II.

Under cofinancing arrangements each NGO is responsible for reporting on and evaluating the projects. The Ministry is kept informed about the status and progress of projects by the annual reporting on the use of funds. Any further requirements concerning evaluation are agreed on a case-by-case basis between the Ministry and NGOs.

The Netherlands

Evaluation is a key tool for the "programme funding" type of co-operation established since 1980. Under the previous system, the four Dutch "umbrella" NGO organisations (CEBEMO, ICCO, NOVIB and HIVOS) had to submit each project for approval. Since 1980, responsibility for project selection has rested exclusively with these organisations, which then submit an annual report to the government. Individual project evaluation continues. Also, six programme evaluations are conducted annually for the government to gather insights on how the programme is carried out. To this end, a programme evaluation is conducted for each cofinancing organisation every two years in each of the main regions (Asia and the Pacific, Africa and the Middle East, and Latin America and the Caribbean). This highly decentralised form of financial co-operation was renewed in 1983 after the initial three-year testing period.

Themes for these programme evaluations are agreed between each of the four umbrella organisations and the government. Also, a common theme for all six evaluations is selected every two years, a recent one being people's participation. Programme evaluations consist of three stages: analysis of project documentation; field missions; the preparation of a report and discussion of its findings. The evaluation team comprises representatives of the Dutch official sector and NGO cofinancing organisation, the partner association in the developing country concerned, and an independent evaluator. Reports are subsequently made public in the language of the country where the projects are located.

Two recent programme evaluations are summarised below. One deals with NOVIB's involvement in Kenya and the second with NOVIB's support for three rural development activities in Burkina Faso and Mali. Both offer insights into relationships between funding NGOs and partner organisations. The second report further attempts to relate priorities to the vulnerable and degraded Sahelian environment and deals with relationships of the implementing NGO with governmental technical services at sub-national level.

The Kenyan report reflects the responsive or active role most appropriate for an external cofunding NGO; and the distribution of project benefits in the many cases when local populations provided voluntary inputs in terms of work, local materials and financial contributions. The poor do not appear to benefit proportionally to their efforts; and women even less. NOVIB's funding in Kenya slackened from 1977 (35 projects supported between 1968 and 1981, with cumulative contributions of approximately $3.2 million, mostly providing basic facilities, e.g., education, health care and water supplies in rural areas). Reasons include NOVIB's perception of itself as mainly a "responsive" organisation, poor experience with co-operative societies in the country, and the paucity of NGO counterparts meeting NOVIB's priorities and criteria. The evaluation team suggests that a more active posture, canvassing for projects and interacting with counterpart organisations rather than just providing funds to project-holders, might lead to better participation of intended beneficiaries.

Self-help projects in Kenya correspond to the national policy of "Harambee" ("co-operation for common good"). Harambee investments in 1966-72 accounted for substantial shares of total national expenditures in education, water supplies, housing, building of churches and community halls, and health care. Yet, focus on the "community", with no special measures for the poor, has meant that the poor who contributed to an investment, for building a school for example, cannot send their children there if they cannot pay the school fees. Although the Harambee concept remained a powerful tool for communal endeavours, in some cases it became distorted and increasing pressure was exerted on the public to make contributions towards activities which chiefly benefitted small groups or individual members of the community. Women, in particular, were heavily involved in providing labour for projects, but largely absent from representative bodies and bypassed by advice, training and funding for income-generating projects notwithstanding the keen interest, work and financial inputs they volunteered to start such projects. [When Two Elephants Fight, it is the Grass that Suffers. NOVIB's Involvement in Kenya, No. 8 of the series of Programme Evaluation of the Cofinancing Programme, The Hague, December 1983.]

The programme evaluation of NOVIB's support for rural development activities in Burkina Faso and Mali deals with three relatively large and long-term programmes, each of which already has a record of trial and error, institutional change, and some reorientation from the previous directive operational style. The report builds on previous evaluations of CEBEMO's activities in the same two countries (1981) and ICCO's in Burkina Faso (1983), respectively centred on community participation and organisational build-up. The central themes of the evaluation of NOVIB in 1984 were the implementation capacity of local partner organisations and their prospects for continuing activities following the phasing out of external assistance. On this latter point, the report's prescription is clearly for a long-term commitment. Two of the three programmes are located in drought-prone areas of Burkina Faso and

Mali where NOVIB's partner, EURO ACTION ACORD (now ACORD), is directly involved with governmental services. (The third project started as a Catholic association in 1965 and continues, as an autonomous foundation, to provide technical services to about 50 villages in an area in western Burkina Faso.) The report diagnoses the situation in the Sahelian area as one of "structural emergency", requiring a skilful blend of emergency and developmental assistance so as to increase resilience in the face of recurring drought and famine. In such a precarious situation the framework for NGOs and other agencies should be provided by a technically and ecologically sound vision of development potential, precluding unintended negative side-effects of specific sector activities (in particular between cattle-raising and cropping). At this broader level, the report raises more questions than it answers, looking to governments, CILSS and the Club du Sahel for appropriate responses. The difficulties due to uncertainty, precariousness and vulnerability are compounded by a lack of trained manpower and of significant local structures for promoting self-help groups. In this context, NOVIB has agreed to support ACORD's activities for relaunching the co-operative movement in a Sahelian area of Mali (6th and 7th regions) and providing staff and funding for a co-ordinating unit within the host-country's administration in Burkina Faso's Sahel region. NOVIB's involvement had started before the latest drought, with support in Burkina Faso for 13 projects and approximately $2.8 million in 1978-83, and 19 projects for approximately $1.5 million in Mali in 1976-83. Virtually all this support was for rural development, including minor components in education, training and health care. Co-operation with governmental services in the new programmes is dictated by necessity for lack of local counterpart NGOs and also corresponds to NOVIB's policy. Reciprocally, co-operation with NGOs is viewed favourably by the government particularly in Burkina Faso, and especially for priority sectors such as water supplies. In Burkina Faso, where NGO flows are substantial, their contribution to the village self-help policy adopted by the government is welcomed. The report notes that large NGOs of the "hand-out" style undermine the common effort of the government and those NGOs which work at developing self-help groups. Greater coherence in approach would be required from NGOs.

Co-operation is also sought by governments of Sahelian countries in order to concentrate their own limited resources on the better-endowed areas in their countries. The report ends on the implications of such a distribution of tasks: NGOs working in outlying, more deprived areas should at the outset prevent the recurrence of famine by launching food security activities which generate income, such as subsidised purchase of cattle. Ways to build up financial self-reliance of beneficiaries over the longer term should be sought. But in the conditions of poverty prevailing in areas such as Mali's 6th and 7th regions self-financing is not an option for a long time to come. On the contrary, external funding of programmes providing services should be foreseen as a long-term proposition. Programming should be responsive to villagers' demands, and therefore flexible. Implications for donors, if they want to support participatory development, are acceptance of multi-year indicative programmes, foreseeing the possibility of changes during programme implementation and related budgetary adjustments.

The constraints which prevail in the programmes supported by NOVIB and ACORD are severe: inadequate practical training, logistics and motivation of host-country services' personnel (often unpaid for months on end); inadequate institutional resources for training villagers; continuing lack of attention to women, their work-burden, their potential contribution to increased income

generation and improved lifestyles. The report questions whether enough
attention is paid to developing a "sound village economy". The co-operative
formula imposed on producers in the Mali project, with the concomitant
government bureaucracy, might be less suited than simpler forms of
co-operation based on mutual interest. Basically, however, the report
underlines the need to change from action based on individuals to action
involving village communities (including women). While it signals some reason
for hope, the report shows the difficult road ahead for self-help groups to
develop in these areas and for their efforts to be rewarded. Many of the
problems raised by this evaluation in relation to organisational issues
continue to attract attention. Some were taken up again in a study of the
dynamics of rural development in other areas of Burkina Faso conducted by the
Club du Sahel in 1987 quoted in Chapter II of this report. [Une seule hache
ne coupe pas un arbre. Soutien NOVIB à des initiatives de développement au
Sahel, Evaluation de programme No 20, The Hague, January 1985.]

The Nordic Countries

In Denmark, findings from seven evaluations undertaken in 1985 show
that projects supporting social services (health and education) have in
general been successful, whereas projects supporting income generating
activities yielded a mixed picture. One main finding of the evaluation is
that project monitoring requires more attention. [Denmark's Development
Assistance 1985, DANIDA, Ministry of Foreign Affairs.]

In Finland a 1984 comprehensive evaluation (including administrative
procedures) of all NGO projects cofinanced by FINNIDA concludes that aid
channelled through NGOs generally reaches people who are most in need.
Official support should be increased to raise the quality and scope of project
impact in social services. Evaluations of individual projects should be more
systematic. Closer co-operation is needed between FINNIDA and NGOs, including
funding NGO personnel training before their departure overseas, using NGO
personnel's advice and experience in FINNIDA's own information and training
activities, and establishing channels for more frequent communication and
discussion. The evaluation team was surprised by the limited number of
permanently paid staff and the amount of unpaid voluntary work at NGOs'
headquarters. For the future, it recommended that the value of this work be
estimated and included in calculation of the NGO-funded share (about 40 per
cent) required of projects presented for cofinancing. More funds should be
made available to NGOs, including missionary organisations, which received
about 70-80 per cent of official cofinancing. Missionary NGOs should take
care to ensure that the services of their projects should not be restricted to
people of their own denominations in the communities in question. In response
to this study, official funding for cofinancing was raised from approximately
$3 million in 1984 to $4 million in 1985 and the number of supported NGOs grew
from 75 to 96. A service centre for NGOs was established in 1985. It will be
responsible among other things for a Finnish Volunteers Service planned to
start in 1986 with NGO co-operation. [Government Supported NGO Development
Co-operation, Summary of Evaluation Report, FINNIDA, 1984.]

In 1985 Norway reported that a survey by NORAD in five of its main
partner countries had prompted further expansion of its support for NGOs.

In 1984, at the government's request, Swedish SIDA conducted a study of the development assistance capacity of NGOs. The report, submitted to the government together with conclusions by the Board of SIDA, was published in 1985. The Board shared the positive evaluation of NGOs' assistance expressed throughout the report. It stressed the need to preserve the identity and independence of NGOs. It noted the capability of larger and more mature NGOs and the need for several other NGOs to strengthen their capacities prior to expanding activities. It saw merit, however, in the enthusiasm and commitment characteristic of new NGOs.

The emphasis in comments by the Board was on the complementarity between official and NGO assistance. Hence, official contributions to NGOs should be expanded from approximately $40 million in fiscal year 1985/86 to $70 million annually during the next three to five years. This increase should take place within the framework of expanded aid aggregates rather than at the expense of other forms of assistance.

In the course of the survey, Swedish NGOs had signalled difficulties in complying with procedures for project application and for reporting to SIDA. SIDA agreed to establish an external service to assist NGOs in preparing applications for cofinancing. The new format for project applications should make it easier to evaluate the project subsequently. The report also recommended an increase in the number of mature NGOs (now limited to two) having authority, on delegation from SIDA, to decide on expenditures of up to SKr 0.5 million of SIDA cofinancing funds allocated to them. The ceiling of amounts thus delegated should be raised to SKr 1 million ($140 000 at 1986 exchange rates). Both measures aim at enhancing flexibility and quick response to changing situations. [Study of the Development Assistance Capacity of Swedish NGOs, Summary in English, SIDA, 1985.]

Switzerland

Switzerland has evaluated a number of NGO projects, often associating nationals of developing countries in these exercises. One evaluation of official emergency aid channelled in part through local self-help organisations in three Sahel countries is referred to in Chapter II.

United Kingdom

In 1982 the Overseas Development Administration (ODA) conducted a survey of its cofinancing scheme. It found that NGO assistance: effectively complements official aid, operates with particular flexibility in areas not usually open to aid agencies, has an effective poverty focus, can be expected to have potential returns quite disproportionate to the resources involved, and is satisfactory in dispensing emergency aid where NGOs may be the only channel of help to people in need. [K.O.H. Osborn and G.A. Armstrong, An Evaluation of the Joint Funding Scheme, ODA, 1982.] A more recent evaluation concerned the Joint Funding Scheme under which ODA provides block grants to four NGOs: Oxfam, the Save the Children Fund, Christian Aid and CAFOD. The evaluation was conducted on the basis of documentation by Mr. R.S. Porter, formerly ODA's Chief Economist. Its main finding was that the systems used by the four agencies for appraising, approving and monitoring their programmes are adequate to ensure that project proposals are carefully examined and that the agencies achieve their stated objectives. ODA grants are used for the purposes specified in the agreement with the Joint Funding Scheme. Mr. Porter made three main recommendations.

a) ODA should agree to meet 75 per cent of the costs instead of 50 per cent.

b) There should be greater flexibility in the size, time span and reporting requirements of projects.

c) Guidelines should be issued by CAFOD and Christian Aid to applicants on the information required in applications so as to make their processing more expeditious.

While the four agencies welcomed the report, neither they nor ODA agreed that the 75:25 per cent ratio would be beneficial. ODA believes that the 50-50 ratio has practical and representational advantages for itself and the agencies. [Joint Funding Scheme: An Evaluation 1986, EV 385/1, Evaluation Department, Overseas Development Administration, London.]

United States

In 1979 US AID commissioned a first comparative evaluation of NGO projects in Kenya and Niger. The study found no consistent relationship between the level of project costs and monetised benefits. Projects with high or moderate impact were where decisions were made by small groups at local level. Marginal impact was associated with a high degree of external NGO involvement in decision-making and with projects initiated by host governments. The chance of a project continuing beyond outside assistance was found to be variable, parallelling the record of development projects supported by bilateral donors. Inadequate attention was paid to training in a number of projects. [A.H. Barclay of Development Alternatives Inc., The Development of Private Voluntary Organisations in Kenya and Niger, Report prepared for US AID, 1979.]

In 1982 Judith Tendler carried out for US AID an evaluation of NGO activities in rural areas based on documentary evidence relating to 75 cases. This study questioned the claims most often made by NGOs as to their comparative advantage. NGOs usually describe themselves as being good at reaching the poor, using participatory processes in project implementation, having innovative and experimental approaches, and carrying out their projects at low cost. The study concluded that many otherwise successful NGO projects did not live up to these claims. Many projects, for instance, did not reach the poor majority or the lowest 40 per cent. Rather than being participatory, they often involved top-down control, though of an enlightened and decentralised nature, often leaving decision-making to local elites. Many NGO projects were not innovative; they extended known service approaches to previously uncovered populations. Further research on both official and NGO projects was needed to assess whether NGOs have a comparative advantage with respect to costs.

The study also considered the impact of projects on the poor when local elites are in control. In projects providing scarce, divisible goods such as seeds, fertilizers, machinery, services, credit, water and electricity connections -- where use by a few means that little is left for the rest -- the poor tended not to benefit. But in projects providing services such as education and health whose use by the privileged few does not reduce their availability to others, a better distribution of benefits was noticed, despite decision-making by elites.

The study by Judith Tendler has influenced subsequent evaluations in other Member countries. The issues it raised still appear to be relevant today. [J. Tendler, Turning PVOs into Development Agencies; Questions for Evaluation, US AID, Evaluation Discussion Paper No. 12, 1982.]

A report to the Administrator of US AID on the role of NGOs in development assistance was published by the US General Accounting Office (GAO) in 1982. A key element in project success was NGOs' implementation capability. Decisive factors which, combined, enhanced capability included experience in the country; collaborative relationships between donor and recipient NGOs; back-up from headquarters; access to required skills; sector experience. The study, which concentrated on the relations between NGOs and US AID, recommended that cofinancing procedures be simplified and better defined, to reflect clarification of the objectives behind official support for NGOs. Finally, the GAO noted that American NGOs were becoming increasingly dependent upon US AID for the financing of their projects. [GAO, Changes Needed to Forge an Effective Relationship between Aid and Voluntary Agencies, Report to the Administrator of US AID, 1982.]

A more recent evaluation of NGO projects by US AID formed part of a general study of small enterprise development. It suggested that NGOs may be able to operate more cost-effectively than other development agencies in meeting the income, employment and productivity needs of poor people in remote areas. [The Evaluation of Small Enterprise Programmes and Projects: Issues in Business and Community Development, US AID, Aid Evaluation Special Study No. 13, 1983.] Other US AID evaluations relating to NGOs and small enterprise development (the PISCES study and Searching for Benefits) are reviewed in Chapter III.

A major evaluation of the performance of NGOs was conducted by US AID at the request of the US House of Representatives and published in 1986. It updated the findings of previous evaluations, with a special focus on NGOs' contribution to AID's development assistance strategy. The impact of NGO projects was assessed against four benchmarks: host-country policies, institutions, technology and the private sector. NGOs' performance in five sectors where they typically operate was also examined: small enterprises, health and nutrition, water and sanitation, agro-forestry and livestock. NGOs were not found to have had any major impact on government policies in three of these. But they had marked and enduring effects on national policies in two sectors at least: primary health care and micro-enterprise. They had demonstrated that rural, community-based primary health care was an effective vehicle for extending coverage and had potential for improving health status. NGOs' support of many years for the informal business sector, from which up to 40-50 per cent of the population in certain countries derive their income, had also encouraged more favourable government policies towards micro-entrepreneurs. The contribution of NGOs in promoting technological change was confirmed. Through local community networks, they helped introduce new technologies and bridge the gap between local official services and the peasant sector. Examples included the introduction of biochemistry and genetics in animal husbandry; oral rehydration, immunisation and child spacing in health care; pipe systems, hand pumps, wells and latrines in water and sanitation.

On institutional development, NGOs had a significant impact at community level, training village workers and even government staff. In most sectors, however, they had very little impact at national level. A number of strengths and weaknesses appeared broadly to characterise NGO activities. Their strengths had already been widely documented: ability to reach the rural poor in unserved areas, promotion of local participation, provision of low-cost services, use of adaptive and innovative technology and ability to maintain an independent status. Major weaknesses included limited replicability, lack of sustainability once outside funding and technical assistance were withdrawn, and absence of broad programming strategies. Too often NGOs preferred to act in isolation rather than pooling resources and insights with other NGOs. Their generally low visibility and independent action hindered the establishment of country-wide programmes. Many projects were designed with limited technical analysis and no collection of baseline data, partly because of low salaries and related insufficiencies in technical and management staff. Together with the paucity of post-project evaluations of impact and effectiveness, the result was too often a "reinvention of the wheel" in subsequent projects. Too few lessons learned were shared, due to scarcity of resources for mechanisms for disseminating information about successes and failures. Many NGOs believed that a shift of funds towards information activities would have detracted from delivery of services and community activities. [Development Effectiveness of Private Voluntary Organisations, Report submitted by US AID to the House of Representatives, February 1986.]

US AID perceives evaluations as a means of gaining insights into comparative advantage and areas where PVO effectiveness might be strengthened. As mentioned already, past evaluations have highlighted small-enterprise development and primary health care. Similar studies have identified a valuable role of PVOs in helping communities preserve their natural resources, through reforestation or land terracing. A new series of evaluations undertaken in 1986-88 will focus on the role of PVOs in strengthening local institutions and in promoting long-term development.

DAC Expert Group on Aid Evaluation

The DAC Expert Group on Aid Evaluation noted in March 1984 that the limited evaluation work available so far tended to show that NGOs have a comparative advantage in addressing basic human needs at the grass-roots level. NGOs may be subject to constraints as to the extent of activities they can administer effectively and therefore to limitations on the volume of resources which can be channelled through them. The Group also recommended that future evaluation work should attempt to identify areas where co-operation with NGOs could increase the quality and impact of aid programmes.

Conclusion

In general, evaluations conducted so far by the official aid agencies of DAC Members, many of them relating to rural development and social service activities, conclude that NGOs have a good record in rural development activities, but they identify a number of recurrent problems which can be summarised as follows. There is a widespread need for better project planning in order to improve the coverage of target groups and to achieve lower project costs which would permit subsequent replication. An improvement in project management would strengthen the economic impact of NGO income-generating activities. They also need to pay more attention to local institution-building, and to adequately training their staff. Moves should be made towards greater collaboration at appropriate levels with services of host-country recipient governments. Two recent NGO initiatives should be signalled. The first is the continuation of activities of the small group of representatives of French NGOs mentioned under Chapter III, devoted to reflection, research and discussion of suitable methods of evaluation. The second is the publication started in the Winter of 1988 of a small magazine by the Swedish NGO "Diakonia", entirely devoted to evaluations of NGO activities (Development Mirror), with articles presented in English, French and Spanish.

A missing element in studies and evaluations of NGOs relates to the human resources which they provide in their activities overseas. How many people from DAC countries work with NGOs in the field? How many of them are volunteers, members of religious orders, recruited staff? In which sectors do they mostly operate and what are their backgrounds? DAC data only show that official funding was extended in 1986 to over 18 000 volunteers, whether of quasi-public bodies or of NGOs, depending on the system adopted by each Member country (see Statistical Annex). But the total of people from DAC countries working in developing countries with NGOs is probably several times higher. Many NGOs typically supply personnel in addition to funding and this probably vast area of lesser-known private technical assistance has not received much attention in the literature so far.

Chapter VI

ROLE OF NGOs IN DEVELOPMENT EDUCATION

Over the past decade NGOs have gained prominence not only as channels for aid but also as major agents in shaping public opinion on development issues. In a few DAC countries, they have increasingly played a role as active pressure groups influencing government policies towards the developing countries.

Together with the media, NGOs provide most of the information received by the public on developing-country issues. The original, and still primary, purpose of their public information activities is to raise funds for their projects overseas. They feel they have a special mission to make people aware that they share responsibility for the developing countries and to encourage feelings of solidarity. By its very nature, fund-raising for emergencies has to portray people as victims. But over the years leading NGOs have progressed from appealing to people's charity to also trying to bring about an understanding of the causes of poverty and problems of development and interdependence. Features of this process are highlighted in Chapter I. In 1983, the DAC organised a meeting on public opinion and aid. Preparatory work showed that in most DAC Members' official aid agencies the bulk of allocations for information is channelled to NGOs for development education and information activities designed by them and meeting established criteria. A DAC meeting planned for 1988 should provide an opportunity for updating information on aid agency co-operation with NGOs in this area. For the while, the present chapter attempts to provide a general view of NGO activities, whether cofinanced or not, rather than specifically focusing on the co-operation extended to them by the public sector.

Types of NGOs involved in development education

Major developmental NGOs have enlarged the scope of their information work beyond the goal of fund-raising and have become involved in broader development education activities. They have established education units within their organisational structure and specialised in the elaboration of educational material including periodicals, magazines, leaflets and books to disseminate information on development. Some operational NGOs have expanded their education departments to sizeable proportions as a measure of the importance they attach to raising public awareness on development issues. This is the case for instance of NOVIB in the Netherlands, which in 1986 employed about 50 people for its development education activities out of a total staff of 130.

In addition, there are NGOs whose exclusive purpose is to widen public perception of developmental issues, and which have no operational activities overseas. Among these non-profit advocacy organisations, some provide development information to a wide public including the school system; e.g., the Centre for World Development Education (CWDE) in the United Kingdom or the United Nations Associations (UNAs) in Norway, Denmark and Sweden. Others perform a role of "think-tanks" and tailor their research to high-level political decision-makers and opinion leaders. These include the Overseas Development Council (ODC) in the United States, the Overseas Development Institute (ODI) in the United Kingdom, and the North-South Institute in Ottawa.

"Think-tanks"

The Overseas Development Council in Washington is a private non-profit organisation established in 1969 for the purpose of increasing American understanding of the economic and social problems confronting the developing countries and of how their development progress is related to US interests. The Council functions as a centre for policy research and analysis, a forum for the exchange of ideas, and a resource for development education. ODC's materials are used by policy-makers in government and Congress, by journalists and by a range of institutions, agencies and action groups concerned about relations with developing countries: corporate and bank management, universities and NGOs. ODC's programmes are funded by foundations, corporations and private individuals. ODC's influential publications include the annual "Agenda" series on "US Foreign Policy and the Third World", and specific sector studies. Some of these have had a wide impact on the perception of problems by developmental agencies: for example the monograph by D.R. Gwatkin, J.R. Wilcok and J.D. Wray Can Health and Nutrition Interventions Make a Difference?, published in 1980 with a foreword by Halfdan Mahler.

The major goal of the Overseas Development Institute (ODI) in London (established in 1960) is to provide information and advice to policy-makers in government, parliament and international institutions so as to influence policies towards developing countries. One of its functions is to provide research and administrative support to an all-party parliamentary group on overseas development which it helped set up in 1984. The intervention of this group was decisive in averting substantial cuts in the 1986 aid programme. A recent publication dealt with developing-country indebtedness. [All-Party Parliamentary Group on Overseas Development, Managing Third World Debt, ODI, London, 1987.] In recent years ODI research has concentrated on agricultural policies, trade issues, EEC relations with developing countries and international finance. When research organisations of this kind enjoy general credibility and maintain high professional standards, they are in a position to play a crucial role in promoting informed debate on development issues. This is particularly true of the ODI in the United Kingdom, which is called upon by politicians to contribute its expertise and knowledge on developing-country issues, as parliamentarians often have neither the staff nor the time for research in depth on development topics.

The North-South Institute in Canada is a non-profit independent corporation established in 1976 to provide professional, policy-relevant research on issues in relations between industrialised and developing countries. Findings and reports are made available to policy-makers, interested groups and the general public. The Institute co-operates with a wide range of Canadian, foreign and international organisations. Examples of the Institute's work include André McNicoll's <u>Drug Trafficking</u> (1983), and a report on rural poverty in Bangladesh, which was subsequently discussed by donor agencies with the government of Bangladesh. A major survey of Canada's NGOs is currently in progress, with support from CIDA, the Government of Alberta, four private foundations and eleven NGOs.

The whole community of NGOs naturally benefits greatly from the results of studies and analyses carried out by these research-oriented non-profit institutions and translates them into a more accessible form for their larger audiences.

In many DAC countries there exist other institutions performing research and publication functions at universities, research centres linked with NGOs, associations and centres for studies on Latin America, Africa and Asia or on specific developmental issues.

Action groups

Formed in some cases by coalitions of NGOs, action groups, often very informal, have long been active in campaigning on issues related to development. This category also comprises innumerable solidarity committees and often unstructured grass-roots movements undertaking such direct action as the organisation of campaigns and boycotts, street demonstrations and lobbying.

For example the Bundeskongress Entwicklungspolitischer Aktionsgruppen (Buko), which acts as a network for 200 action groups in Germany, launched three major national campaigns in the 1980s which met with some success. It challenged in turn the marketing strategy of the pharmaceutical industry in developing countries and the role of German agribusiness corporations in rural development; and it campaigned against the export of military equipment to developing countries. In Europe these campaigns usually spread beyond national borders and link at an international level through network organisations such as ICDA based in Brussels (see Chapter I) or NIO Youth in Amsterdam.

NIO Youth co-ordinated an international campaign on the least developed countries which involved about 30 NGOs from 20 different countries, on the occasion of the Mid-term Review of the Substantial New Programme of Action (SNPA) in Geneva in 1985. The thrust of the campaign was to mobilise popular support in order to persuade governments to fulfil the commitments undertaken towards LLDCs at the Paris Conference in 1981.

Scope and contents of NGO development education work

Unlike the information provided by aid agencies, NGOs' education work is not confined to information on official aid programmes but tends to encompass a broad range of North-South and development issues. NGOs' interest in these broader international development issues stems from the acknowledgement that changes in North-South relationships in such sectors as trade would have greater impact on many developing countries than private or official aid. Currently, developing-country indebtedness figures prominently among themes of NGOs' information activities.

Operational NGOs with recognised professional experience in development go to great lengths to explain the many factors affecting development prospects to the general public through newsletters, magazines and other publications. The 1985 annual report of Action Aid, a British child sponsorship and community development agency, gave comprehensive coverage of topics as diversified as: poverty, community participation, soil erosion, women's status, water, disease, malnutrition, training and credit schemes. The issues were presented in an educational way, understandable to lay readers, without being too simplistic. Practical knowledge of developing countries through the financing of projects is generally recognised to be an asset in development education work in the home country, as the experience gained mitigates the danger of excessive abstraction and ideological simplification.

Some NGOs which have undertaken to study development issues have gradually become more sophisticated in their analyses of the causes and mechanisms of underdevelopment. In recent years, they have addressed the complex web of causes of famine in Africa and the search for solutions. They stress the man-made and structural roots of the persistent food crisis, linking them with such factors as environmental degradation, agricultural decline, financial disincentives, debt burden, world commodity prices, distortions in exchange rates, etc. [See for example Tony Hill, Catholic Institute for International Relations (United Kingdom), "NGOs and Africa's Crisis: A Discussion of the Experience in the United Kingdom and Strategic Issues for Future Work", working paper for "NGOs and Africa: A Strategy Workshop", UN-NGLS, Geneva, 14th-17th November 1985.] With respect to debt, structural adjustment programmes and the plight of the poor, Oxfam shared its experience and analysis of these situations, in Zambia and elsewhere, with other NGOs at the September 1987 workshop in Oxford [See UN-NGLS Geneva, UN-NGO Workshop on Debt, Adjustment and the Needs of the Poor (11-20 September 1987), Oxford, Final Report, 1987]. The final statement of NGO representatives to that workshop represented a platform for further work by NGOs (available in published form in the supplement to Vol. 15 of the World Development journal, Autumn 1987).

In their development education NGOs' activities are also increasingly concerned with broader issues such as the defence of human rights, disarmament and the protection of the environment and their implications for developing countries. An impressive number of NGOs have extended their development education activities to active participation in solidarity groups concerned with victims of dictatorships, apartheid, forced eviction or the infringement of rights of ethnic minorities.

Current acceptance of development education

While specialists are wary of trying to define development education precisely, the current acceptance of the term reflects the enlarged scope of NGOs' concerns. For example, New Zealand established a new Development Education Programme in 1986 to provide small grants and matching contributions to NGOs. The official formulation used in enunciating the goals of the programme correspond closely to the way many NGOs would describe development education.

"Development education is more than just information about development co-operation. It is about the process of development itself, what aids it, what inhibits it and the linkages involved. (Its) central purpose is to increase awareness and to develop an understanding of the linkages between the common interests and concerns in communities in New Zealand and the developing world. (It) seeeks to focus upon the underlying causes and structures of underdevelopment (poverty and powerlessness) and to encourage active participation by New Zealanders in their elimination. (It) helps New Zealanders to discover the relevance of third world conditions to their own lives and an understanding of the causes of poverty in their own nation and neighbourhood. Working with disadvantaged people and minority groups can lead to the realisation that these are in fact global problems requiring global solutions." While increased understanding by New Zealanders of the value of international development co-operation programmes is one of the goals of the programme, others include "respect for women and men of all cultures", "the links between affluence and poverty", "the interrelationship between peace and development", and counteracting "community prejudice, including racism and sexism".

Means for disseminating information

Efforts by NGOs to promote consciousness-raising and information campaigns in their home countries to increase public awareness of the problems of developing countries take a variety of forms, as illustrated by the following examples.

-- Production of published material such as magazines, newsletters, pamphlets, brochures, country profiles, fact-sheets, books etc. Central to the ODI's publication programme, for instance, are its widely praised "briefing papers". These are fact-sheets averaging four pages each and providing accessible information and analysis on development issues. A survey of their readership in 1985 revealed that they are read at the highest levels of government and widely appreciated by politicians, academics and the business community.

-- Presentation of films, video and slides. In the United Kingdom a group of NGOs has established a film company to produce documentaries on development, the International Broadcasting Trust (IBT), to help popularise development issues. Too many television programmes emphasize development failures, so IBT has selected cases of community participation in projects that have been successful. Many NGOs produce audio-visual aids.

-- Organisation of lectures, conferences, seminars and briefings. An important element of Christian Aid's development education work is to extend invitations to guests from developing countries to visit the United Kingdom and give talks on their personal experience and the situation in their country. To arrange lectures NGOs often rely on local organisers and education officers who visit schools, churches and clubs around the country to give education sessions.

-- Informing the media. NGOs generally attach great importance to the way the press and broadcasters present Third World issues and some provide briefings for this purpose. In Canada and the United

States, returned volunteers and NGOs are often at the origin of programmes by local television stations and newspapers on developing countries. Improving coverage of Africa by the media is currently high on the NGO agenda, as illustrated by various initiatives mentioned in the last section of this chapter.

-- A supportive role is played by several UN agencies and bodies. In particular, since October 1985 UN-NGLS in Geneva publishes "Go-Between", a newssheet providing information on UN and other events and publications of interest to NGOs. It has also published useful directories of development education periodicals and of NGOs active in development education (1).

Role of NGOs in stimulating development education in schools

Together with the aid agencies and education authorities, many NGOs are also instrumental in introducing development education into schools in DAC countries. The following examples highlight activities.

The Centre for World Development Education (CWDE) is the leading NGO in the United Kingdom exclusively dedicated to providing materials and methodological guidance for development education to a very broad public. It is neither an active pressure group nor a research institute. Its role, rather, is to provide what could be called objective information about development problems. About half of CWDE's work is in formal education with schools and colleges where the Centre concentrates mainly on helping teachers who include development issues in their curricula by providing them with background material, teaching methods and computer software.

In France, various ministerial instructions have authorised as from 1981 the introduction of development education in schools. Most of the activities are still experimental and organised spontaneously by interested teachers and most of the material is provided by NGOs. The designation of a day as "Third World day" provides a stimulus. Materials and methods have been elaborated by Frères des hommes, Peuples solidaires, CFCF, CCFD and many others. Activities are also conducted in agricultural schools, most of them private (Catholic) with support from specialised NGOs networks such as SOLAGRAL and RONGEAD. The latter also organises debates with farmers' associations on such controversial issues as the Common Agricultural Policy and its repercussions on food self-sufficiency and cereals exports in developing countries.

MS (Mellemfolkeligt Samvirke) in Denmark is the NGO which operates the official volunteer programme for DANIDA. In the framework of its development education activities MS publishes a monthly magazine, Kontact, which has become the largest periodical on development topics issued in Nordic countries and is primarily targeted to students in high schools and colleges. In addition, MS publishes a quarterly magazine for grammar school pupils to give them the opportunity to become familiar with international problems. Typical subjects dealt with in these magazines in recent years include food supply problems, refugees, disarmament, the situation in Southern Africa and Central America. The offices of MS house the most complete and comprehensive library on development issues in the country. MS also publishes more than a dozen books every year for the education system.

Danchurchaid is the only Danish NGO making its own films on development. It has a collection of 50 films in its education department which are regularly shown in schools and occasionally also broadcast on national television. In its films, Danchurchaid departs from the traditional appeals to compassion, attempting instead to educate students to the intricate and complex causes of underdevelopment (low prices of commodities, heavy debt burden, high cost of the arms race, EEC food policies, etc.). It also attempts to make the broad public feel the problems of development in a way it can find meaningful. A recent film on Africa, for instance, draws a comparison of daily life in two communities, in Denmark and Kenya.

The United Nations Association of Norway (UNA) receives a third of government funds allocated to development education activities (about $600 000 in 1984). It gives particular emphasis to development education in the school system, where it has obtained a firm footing. In Norway there is a certain amount of competition among NGOs to produce the most attractive and interesting educational material for schools. Opinion polls in fact indicate the crucial importance of school education with regard to young people's attitudes towards development aid. In the 16-19 year age group, as many as 93 per cent of young Norwegians support assistance to developing countries and almost none are against.

Ireland is the DAC country where relative to national income and to the development co-operation budget the joint effort of government and NGOs in development education is the highest. Special mention should be made of Trocaire's lively and informative three-volume series for schools and youth groups Dialogue for Development (one of these, first published in 1983, had four reprints by 1986) and its co-operation with the British Christian Aid in producing a fourth companion volume (2).

Networks on development education in school curricula

There exists a European Development Education Curriculum Network (EDECN), promoting development education in schools through conferences, the production of an inventory ("Who's Who in Development Education in the European Community") and research with support by the CEC. Its Dutch affiliate, CEVNO, itself a specialised network, has acquired prominence in activities in schools.

In December 1986, the numerous NGOs involved in development education in schools in Italy established a national network on an experimental basis. In addition to facilitating exchange, this association, which groups NGOs of the different ideological families, aims at contributing to creating an informed movement of public opinion on issues relating to Italy's official development co-operation.

Although at present there are many unco-ordinated efforts in the production of materials for schools, an encouraging example of a more systematic approach is provided by an NGO specialising in audio-visual material for secondary schools [GRAD (Groupe européen de réalisations audio-visuelles sur le développement)], which also adapts and translates audio-visual aids from other sources for use in several French-speaking countries.

Role of NGOs as pressure groups

Many NGOs combine development education addressed to the general public with lobbying aimed at decision-makers. In most DAC countries, NGOs lead the public debate on both the volume and the quality of aid. They have traditionally been strong supporters of increased allocations to the aid budget of their countries and resisted cuts. They are recognised as constituting the strongest domestic lobby in DAC countries to meet the aid volume target of 0.7 per cent of GNP as ODA and more recently the sub-target of 0.15 per cent of GNP as official aid to the least developed countries.

In recent years, the NGO community in several DAC countries has undertaken campaigns to maintain or increase the volume of aid and improve its quality in terms of programmes addressing poverty. Endorsing the "basic needs" or "poverty-focused" strategies that characterise their own project work, NGOs in some countries challenge the more commercial and political components of development assistance, engaging in critical analysis of official aid programmes and pressing for reforms of government policies towards developing countries through lobbying tactics and national campaigns. In several European countries, annual debates on the aid budget in parliament have constituted a major lobbying opportunity, as illustrated by the few examples given below. From the perspective of NGO strategy, one of the most important developments, particularly in Europe, is increased collaboration amongst NGOs in campaigns and lobbying activities, giving more weight to their demands and proposals.

NGOs underline their common concern about constraints to development such as structural issues in trade and developing countries' indebtedness. In Europe, the concern of NGOs in the area of trade include EEC protectionism against developing-country manufactured exports, particularly textiles, greater support for measures that address the problem of terms of trade in commodities, and restrictions on the use of EEC agricultural surpluses for non-emergency food aid. In 1985, for example, NGOs from seven European countries joined in a signature campaign on "the right of populations to feed themselves". Signatories asked national governments and the European Commission to devote 4 per cent of the value of non-emergency food aid to funding rural development and food self-sufficiency programmes benefitting the poorer population groups and to assisting small farmers' associations. On the issue of debt, the dialogue of NGOs with governments currently focuses on cancelling the bilateral debt of the least developed countries. This activity has had considerable impact in the Nordic countries. For developing countries other than the least developed, NGOs ask for a more sensitive handling of the debt problem, with extended grace periods, interest-rate reductions and upper limits for debt service ratios.

In addition to scrutiny of their national aid programmes, NGOs also follow major international negotiations and conferences which serve as rallying points, such as UNCTAD, negotiations over successive Lomé Conventions, GATT and SNPA. They send observers who try to persuade the delegates of the industrialised countries to respond more favourably to the demands of developing countries. In the 1970s NGOs generated support for UNCTAD conferences and the concept of a New International Economic Order. In the 1980s, however, NGOs came to recognise the utopian nature of the latter issue. Most developmental NGOs changed strategy and concentrated their efforts on more immediate issues, including campaigns on regulating publicity for baby foods as alternatives to breast-feeding, and on other issues with implications for developing countries, such as pharmaceuticals, pesticides, and activities of multinational corporations.

Examples of lobbying for ODA

Increased collaboration among NGOs in lobbying activities was one of the most significant developments in the United Kingdom in the 1980s. The most visible initiative in this respect was the mass demonstration in 1985 which involved almost all British NGOs in the mobilisation of 20 000 supporters gathered at Westminster to seek changes in British policies towards the developing countries. Demonstrators urged the government to take appropriate action for famine prevention in the four areas of food aid, trade, official development assistance, and debt.

Lobbying is an essential aspect of the activities of the four umbrella NGOs in the Netherlands (CEBEMO, ICCO, NOVIB and HIVOS), which, as cofinancing organisations, receive grants from the government both for the funding of projects overseas and for development education activities. They participate in monthly meetings with officials from the Directorate-General of Development Co-operation and seek to orient Dutch aid policy towards greater support for the least developed countries and underprivileged population groups. Their experience in field projects and their links with academic research give them respected expertise in discussing their country's aid programme. At the level of the European Commission as well, they try to exert pressure for policies in favour of the poorest groups in developing countries and with respect to sensitive regions in Southern Africa and Central America.

In Belgium, most NGOs are members of one of the two national centres of co-operation (French and Flemish).. These two umbrella organisations (CNCD and NCO) are particularly active in the co-ordination of fund-raising campaigns and lobbying. In a particularly successful case, Belgian NGOs with support from religious leaders and city mayors were able to bring before Parliament an appeal of 77 Nobel Prize holders for ending world hunger. As a result of the campaign, in 1983 parliament virtually unanimously approved the establishment of a Survival Fund of $200 million for development assistance to developing countries.

In Sweden, NGOs have been prominent in bringing public pressure to bear on the government to increase the volume of aid. In 1983 for the first time the government proposed a freeze of the aid budget. This decision met with fierce opposition from religious NGOs, which enlisted the support of the NGO community at large and succeeded in inducing the government to reverse its decision and increase development allocations. Swedish NGOs, like most European NGOs, are also relentless critics of aspects of aid policy which may grant hidden commercial advantages. On the occasion of the presentation of the aid budget to Parliament in 1985, the NGO lobby gathered its supporters in front of Parliament for three consecutive days, this time to protest against the increased weight of commercial considerations in aid. Diakonia, the Swedish Missionary Council, and other church-related organisations constitute a strong pressure group that decision-makers cannot ignore. While receiving substantial financial support from SIDA, these NGOs are forefront critics of Swedish aid policies whenever the government tries to reduce the volume or the poverty focus of its commitment to development assistance. They have otherwise consistently defended the aid programme and advocated its further build-up.

In Denmark, five or six prominent NGOs usually take the lead in putting pressure on the government when its commitment to a high level and quality of aid is at stake. Through their affiliated organisations these NGOs represent a large segment of the Danish population, adding weight to their petitions and interventions. NGOs, church organisations and the labour unions lobbied successfully in 1983 to prevent cuts in the aid budget. As a result of the broad consensus which exists in Denmark between the government and the NGO community with regard to the main features of development assistance, the NGO movement -- aside from a few exceptional cases of vigorous reaction -- generally tends to play a quiet role of dialogue and careful scrutiny, with fewer confrontational features than in the United Kingdom. In Finland, the "Percentage Movement" has been influential in the country's commitment to reach the 0.7 per cent ODA target by the end of this decade. Supporters of this movement commit themselves to devote 1 per cent of their income to development co-operation. These contributions are channelled to various NGOs.

Major current and planned events

Much of the current focus is on the "image of Africa", trying to adjust the message conveyed by NGOs and the media in ways which convey some feeling for Africans' own efforts, rather than continue to portray them as helpless victims. A major meeting on these matters was convened in Berne in June 1987 by the Swiss government in liaison with UN agencies, inviting other bilateral donors and NGOs. The Berne meeting provided an opportunity to study some of the factual reasons for inadequate coverage of Africa in newspapers and on television (e.g., high travel and living costs, the fading out of well-informed "stringers" of previous years as press freedom was narrowed in many countries, the paucity of in-country reliable sources of information and the close scrutiny of what is "news" exercised by budget-conscious foreign editors). It was also learned that Canadian NGOs had joined forces in 1986 as "Partnership Africa Canada" (PAC) primarily to strengthen host-country partner organisations under CIDA's large new five-year "Africa 2000" programme. Canadian NGOs represented in PAC decided to devote to information within Canada 10 per cent (C$ 7.5 million) of the Africa 2000 programme's 50 per cent share to be channelled through them.

A conference was held in Rome (on 1-5 February 1988) under the aegis of FAO's Freedom from Hunger/Action for Development on "Africa's image". The conference was supported by the Italian authorities, associating three Italian NGOs (Terra Nuova, Crocevia and CRIC of Reggio Calabria) with NGOs from six other European countries (SOS Faim from Belgium, Trocaire from Ireland, Oxfam, the Comité français contre la faim, Deutsche Welthungerhilfe and Danchurchaid). The meeting reviewed findings from research on the image of Africa conveyed over the past three years by the media and NGOs in each of the European countries represented. Studies were also conducted in six African countries on how local organisations reacted to the famine emergency and other topics to provide information with a better balanced view of African efforts. Activities of self-help organisations such as ORAP in Zimbabwe and NAAM in Burkina Faso featured prominently. A report on this conference is being prepared by Terra Nuova.

North-South interdependence and solidarity is the theme of a major information campaign mainly aimed at youth which the Council of Europe is launching in its 21 member countries, with support from governments, the European Commission, the European Parliament, NGOs and other bodies. Preparations started in March 1987 and the campaign will take place in April and May 1988. The campaign is based on seven major issues, in an attempt to increase awareness also on some more controversial aspects where sector interests may currently diverge between developed and developing countries. The themes relate to trade, agriculture, natural resources and the environment, debt and financial transfers, the volume and quality of aid, employment, and socio-cultural relationships, including human rights.

NGOs are associated with initiatives of the national committees established by each member country of the Council of Europe and also design special initiatives with CEC support in the twelve EEC countries. One initiative is a whole train, equipped jointly by several NGOs with support from the CEC. Five wagons will present information on themes of the Council of Europe's campaign. One is equipped for film shows, and two will be a temporary home to returned European volunteers and developing-country students to engage in dialogue with young people in the cities where the train will stop. The train will move across mainly middle-sized European cities including Rome, Strasbourg, Luxembourg, Brussels and Madrid between April and October 1988.

Representatives of NGOs from developing countries at the World Development/ODI London symposium of March 1987 referred to previously [cf. World Development, Special Issue of Autumn 1987, No. 15, Supplement] made a strong plea to NGO representatives from DAC countries to use their leverage with informed public opinion and governments towards widening perception of interdependence and influencing official policies along directions more favourable to development. This plea was a central theme in the 1987 annual forum of INTERACTION, the umbrella organisation which currently groups most developmental PVOs in the United States. For a number of reasons, PVOs in the United States have been less involved than Canadian or European NGOs in a policy dialogue on such broader issues. (Some PVOs, however, notably those which are primarily concerned with poverty and environmental issues, play an active role in testimonies at United States legislative committees to influence concern with the poor, the environment, health assistance in legislation related to funding of US AID and the World Bank's IDA.) The central messages from the London meeting were reviewed by the INTERACTION forum and reflected in its news-sheet and several of the forum's workshops dealt with public policy issues and development education. This interest is expected to lead to greater focus on development education by US PVOs in the future.

Conclusions

There is no doubt that NGOs' role in information and development education is impressive, although it appears to be more effective in relation to official development co-operation policies, even in instances where stances are confrontational, in DAC countries where relations between the public sector and NGOs are closer and where opportunities for dialogue and reciprocal questioning are institutionalised. A series of studies conducted for the Task Force on Concessional Flows of the Development Committee of the World Bank and

IMF in 1986 found that in the majority of European donor countries it is the activities of NGOs that have the major impact in generating support for aid and for maintaining a high profile of development issues before the public and national parliaments. ["Aid for Development: The Key Issues. Supporting Materials for the Report of the Task Force on Concessional Flows", Development Committee, No. 8, The World Bank, Washington DC, 1986.] The Report of the Development Committee's Task Force found, therefore: "There is a special scope for continuing and enhancing the active development education role of non-governmental organisations, especially those that are engaged in development work overseas. We call on both bilateral and multilateral aid agencies to work closely with these organisations to further better understanding of development problems and the role of aid in alleviating them." ["Report of the Task Force on Concessional Flows", Development Committee, No. 7, The World Bank, Washington DC, 1985.]

A few points may be mentioned in concluding this overview. As noted already, most official aid agencies extend cofinancing contributions to NGOs to support their development education activities. The Commission of the European Communities does so as well. These amounts, however, are on a considerably smaller scale than contributions for development activities in developing countries. Many NGOs therefore contribute funding for their information and educational activities from their own resources. Given competing demands, this may raise serious problems for NGOs which depend mainly on privately-raised resources.

In development education as in other activities NGOs maintain an independent stance with respect to governments and, naturally, in their campaigns tend to intervene more on issues that present problems than on others. Their interventions in public debate discourage complacency, and may in some instances question official policies on aid or other matters. Most DAC Member governments accept this and some leave full latitude to NGOs as to the choice of contents of the information for which public funding is used.

There are dangers in some of the stances of NGOs in development education. They may be quantitatively misleading, they may contribute to a globally negative image of official aid, they may create developing-country stereotypes and they may build up a feeling of guilt in audiences. NGOs' fund-raising may induce the public to equate all "real" aid with the NGOs, and to remain unaware of their quantitative significance relative to official aid. Opinion polls in some DAC countries in past years have shown that substantial fractions of the population are convinced that the volume of aid from NGOs is larger than that of official aid. Some NGOs, in the images of the developing countries that they portray, have a propensity for stereotypes, with a good-and-bad vision of the world. In some cases, "bad" features of NGOs' favourite countries, such as a need for policy changes or for raising of administrative standards, will be skipped over. The tendency to favour certain developing countries has been analysed, for instance for French NGOs (3). Another danger is that the virtues claimed for NGOs in their fund-raising publicity are sometimes presented in the form of a contrast with official aid, which may lead to blanket criticism of official aid. The danger is reinforced by the fact that the failures of the NGOs, being mainly on a relatively small scale, receive less publicity than do those of the official agencies. Thus there is a risk that NGOs may play into the hands of more radical critics of aid, whether from the left or the right. Also, some NGO campaigns cultivate a feeling of guilt in their audiences on events which are in fact beyond the realm of these audiences to correct or modify. As noted by the author of a major study of development education in the early 1980s, guilt feelings are a poor basis for spreading the messages of solidarity beyond restricted circles (4).

The gulf thus opened up between the NGOs and official agencies is to be regretted, is probably often unintended, and is in any case belied by the growing co-operation between the two. To the professional aid administrator, the stances taken by NGOs sometimes appear to be poorly based, with inadequate and often naive analysis, and confrontational in tone. Yet the issues identified by the NGOs are often real ones -- the anomaly, for instance, of a world encumbered with food surpluses amid starvation -- even though the perspectives within which such issues are seen may differ. In their own way, NGOs are constantly trying to bridge the distances between the realities in poor countries and what people in DAC countries see and hear.

Given the impact and importance of their information work, ways of achieving more consistent quality deserve consideration, in terms of what both the public sector and NGOs themselves can do. In their advocacy role for development issues pertaining to aid, institutionalised opportunities for closer and more continued dialogue with the official aid agencies hold potential for better-grounded information work, with a greater understanding over time of aid policies and programmes. This implies a willingness on the part of the aid agencies to undertake a dialogue which may have its asperities. Some DAC Members have taken this course (see Chapter IV). Benefits would be reciprocal, as such opportunities would also contribute to greater transparency of public-sector activities and thus ultimately through NGOs' impact on sections of public opinion to stronger and more widespread support for aid.

On the NGO side, their fragmentation is probably an important constraint. They have successfully mounted a number of joint campaigns. Particularly in their work on broader complex issues affecting development, there would be advantages in a more widespread sharing of the analytical capacity which exists in some NGOs and research institutions, and in gearing this capacity to adequate research on these issues. Credibility of NGO information work and impact on decision-makers would be more sustained. To some extent there may be problems of resources involved here as well which may deserve consideration by the public sector.

A major difficulty which NGOs are facing now is their wish to present a more positive image of developing countries' populations' own efforts and how this may affect the outcome of fund-raising appeals. The involvement and to some extent identification of local communities within DAC countries through "twinning" arrangements with defined partners in developing countries may provide one of the answers to this problem. Still, the challenge of maintaining a balance between the presentation of progress achieved in developing countries and the needs that remain to be met is likely to prove very difficult indeed. How it can be done without weakening the case for resource mobilisation remains to be seen.

1. UN-NGLS/Geneva: Development Education: The State of The Art, 1986; Directory of Development Education Periodicals: NGOs in Western Europe, Australia and New Zealand, International NGOs, Networks of NGOs, UN System, Governmental and Intergovernmental Organisations, 1987; Development Education: A Directory of Non-governmental Practitioners. NGOs in Western Europe, Australia and New Zealand, International NGOs, International (North-South) NGO Networks, 1987.

2. TROCAIRE, Dialogue for Development, A Survey of Some Global Issues, Book I, 1983, Book II, 1985, and Teacher's Handbook, 1984; and It's not Fair! A Handbook on World Development for Schools and Youth Groups, Irish edition prepared by Trocaire and Christian Aid, Dublin, 1984.

3. An analysis of the "discourse" of French NGOs in their information and educational work has been conducted by Christian Joly, Organisations non gouvernementales françaises et développement, Economica, Paris, 1985.

4. Pierre Pradervand, Development Education, the 20th Century Survival and Fulfilment Skill, a report to the Swiss Federal Department of Foreign Affairs, Berne, 1982 (covers development education in Belgium, Canada, Germany, the Netherlands, Norway, Sweden, the United Kingdom). A briefer version was published in the February 1982 issue of Entwicklung-Développement, the development magazine of the Swiss Federal Department of Foreign Affairs.

Chapter VII

CONCLUSIONS

Examples given from experience and evaluations may convey some idea of the difficulties NGOs face both in their operations and in fund-raising. Some of these difficulties are inherent in the process of development, and will be encountered by any development agency -- NGOs, official aid agencies, and the governments of the developing countries themselves. The NGO sector also has specific constraints and weaknesses of its own. Some are outlined in the evaluations summarised in Chapter V. Others derive from the generally small size of NGOs and their activities and the element of uncertainty in their funding, compared with the scale and dimensions of poverty problems in the world today. In addition, over the past ten years or so many NGOs have come to include among their tasks an understanding of broader trends and economic relationships between developed and developing countries, both to inform their constituencies and to have an influence on the whole range of policies which affect development. These are huge challenges. In a world where so many factors induce feelings of impotence, indifference or escapism, NGOs maintain and publicise a vision of mankind as one and are among those who act to make life more tolerable for more people. For these reasons, virtually all public-sector institutions responsible for development co-operation have come to view them as partners and to feel that their efforts deserve support.

In this multifaceted and changing context, conclusions mainly from the viewpoint of relations of official aid agencies with NGOs as reflected in DAC work can only be offered as one element among others, together with messages signalled from other fora and new directions sought by professionals and researchers with a long record of relevant experience.

Conclusions are sketched under two main headings:

-- Changing relationships between NGOs in the North and the South;

-- The search for improved complementarities within broader development policies and programmes.

But first it should perhaps be admitted that this report, in its selective focus -- on self-help and income-generating initiatives, and on development education -- could not aim at comprehensive coverage. The issues that might have been covered more fully include, among others, the following:

-- NGOs' work and the growth of host-country NGO networks in Latin America, often supported by domestic policy analysis and research centres such as DESCO (Centro de Estudios y Promocion del Desarrollo) in Peru;

130

-- NGOs' experiences in urban settings and the reversion in many urban programmes in recent years to caritative components such as soup-kitchens to care for immediate needs of some urban groups' exacerbated poverty;

-- NGO activities in family planning and the promotional role of the sector's lead agency, the London-based International Planned Parenthood Federation (IPPF), providing support for host-country affiliates, many in developing countries and many of which have acquired national significance (1);

-- The potential of twinning arrangements and decentralised co-operation (involving regional and municipal administrations as well as states, in countries which have a federal government), and the role of NGOs in such arrangements;

-- The deepening nexus of environmental and human rights concerns, including minorities' rights, with NGOs' development and advocacy work (2).

The information provided in the report does, it is hoped, provide a picture of the diversity of NGOs and the range of their activity, of current issues of common concern and the emerging dialogue between NGOs and official institutions on the central issue of poverty. The discussion of co-operation between aid agencies and NGOs shows the value attached by aid agencies to the autonomy of NGOs.

Changing relationships between NGOs in the North and the South

Improved partnership with NGOs of the South and its implications for strengthening viable autonomous local institutions as against direct implementation and short-term achievements should remain a central and priority goal. For some time already, it has been widely recognised that desirable directions for NGOs in the North over the longer term include less direct implication in project initiatives, design and implementation, the maintenance of a funding and supportive role, and enhanced advocacy for improving the chances of developing countries' poor majorities. Much still remains to be done in practice in these directions.

Many external NGOs still look upon local initiatives as "their" projects, rather than evolving strategies aimed at strengthening independent partners that will ultimately develop in their own way. Yet, strong and autonomous local initiatives can develop over time to meet more needs and make use of more potential than external NGOs can ever expect to do. These limitations in perception apply, beyond the developmental NGOs with which this report is mostly concerned, also to welfare agencies. Welfare is a broad term covering activities focused on human resources, such as child care, nutrition and education. Its importance cannot be overestimated. In these areas as well, a voluntary agency may limit its views to its own "project" -- which can be a valuable one -- or it may adopt (or agree to become part of) a strategy whereby even limited activities can have relevance for the broader context. In the latter case, it may undertake or stimulate research, seek co-operation with other entities, endeavour to promote programmes to meet the real requirements. Several child sponsorship agencies for example have taken a step in this direction by engaging in community development activities beyond assistance for the individual child. To be able to provide effective support to the development of local organisations, a number of existing NGOs would need for reasons of size to accept pooling or linking their efforts with others. The encouraging trends of the past ten years along these lines, exemplified by several NGOs' joint funding of ACORD or by consortia such as ECAD in Europe, PACT in the United States -- and more recently the Asian NGO Coalition (ANGOC), a network of NGOs working for rural development in several countries of South and South-East Asia -- deserve to be pursued.

Some donor NGOs fear that abandoning the project approach will result in fewer resources. They highlight their projects in fund-raising activities and obtain official cofinancing for precise projects. In its most strident form, the otherwise positive current tension over increasing resources for NGOs of the South is expressed in terms of rights: a right by the latter to uncontrolled access to resources of donor NGOs, and a right of donor NGOs to "compensation" for the funds that would no longer be channelled through them. The reasoning in such arguments is difficult to follow. They mainly seem to indicate the extent to which dependence in funding may lead to an exclusive focus on money. The supportive functions of donor NGOs are not limited to acting as a channel of funds and, reciprocally, the use of external funds should be appraised with discernment (3). NGO constituencies in DAC countries may be encouraged to identify themselves with the joint efforts of partner organisations, rather than with a traditional project implemented from the outside. Official donors also should provide a larger share of their contributions to donor NGOs in more flexible fashion, as is appropriate for institution-building processes. This point comes out strongly from relevant recent research, some of which has been presented in Chapters II, III and V.

Another implication of re-orienting NGO strategies as more of the initiative and implementation in the field can be taken over by their partners in the South is the increasing need for qualified personnel to perform the specialised tasks for which donor NGOs will continue to be needed in a supportive capacity: in management, training, market research, etc.

Among developmental NGOs, those most inclined so far to support independent local organisations appear to be large NGOs which limit the bulk of their activity to a funding role. Examples include the Dutch umbrella organisations, Germany's Misereor, the Ford Foundation, and, usually on a smaller scale, Oxfam. Smaller NGOs, however, may also adopt institution-building values and strategies, as exemplified by International Voluntary Service in the United States and by Australian NGOs' views on priorities for their aid in the Pacific (4). These stress activities that favour decentralisation in decision-making, regionalisation, localisation of planning, the support and strengthening of local-level institutions, the establishment of information exchange and communication channels, and raising the consciousness of populations for participation in local institutions and action.

In some cases, limitations to seeing partners as potentially autonomous local institutions occur along a religious divide. For example some church-linked organisations recognise only a religious authority as their partner, and their programmes within local communities address only the specific group of the faithful rather than the community as such. Limitations of this kind, however, are found in other types of donor NGO as well.

The same considerations apply in some cases to NGOs of the South. Some tend to exert excessive control (e.g., administration-intensive scrutiny of individual loans), to create "their" groups at local level and to overstretch their capacity in trying themselves to design local multi-sector development programmes. Research suggests that greater impact would be achieved by strategies aimed at creating local groups (these may coincide with existing administrative jurisdictions) and supporting them, while also favouring other horizontal and vertical linkages, rather than exerting detailed control and seeking agency autarchy.

Accountability to their constituents and donors is one of the reasons advanced by NGOs of the North for maintaining their own distinctive projects rather than investing in the nurturing of local partners. Yet, accountability is not incompatible with the more flexible funding suited to the development of local groups. Indeed, the need for even greater financial accountability in promoting self-help movements was stressed by CEBEMO's study quoted in Chapter III. At the London meeting of the World Development/ODI in March 1987, Charles Elliott, former director of Christian Aid, noted that it is as easy to mock the Weberian virtues as it is to neglect the fact that local NGOs need honesty and competence as sources of strength to become effective agents of change in their environment. Some larger European NGOs have developed models of co-operation with partners in the South demonstrating that the financial accountability and transparency required by NGOs vis-à-vis their private and official donors in DAC countries are compatible with flexibility and decentralisation in the field. Farmers' and women's groups in West Africa whose training currently centres so strongly on accounting and management remind us that transparency is also needed for the ultimate intended beneficiaries to exercise control from the local level upwards through the chain of representative associations.

Improved management should not relate only to accounting for the aid received, but to all the resources available to grass-roots movements and their vertical organisations including their own efforts and resources.

Donor NGOs can provide valuable assistance to improve management, including training. A major obstacle in this perspective is competition among aid sources, including NGOs, reflected in different forms of aid offered to the same local institutions for the same purposes. There is no reason why a local women's group should insist on funding the purchase of sheep through a reimbursable loan or men should volunteer their labour for digging if yet another donor offers the same goods free. This competition is currently stronger in Africa South of the Sahara than in other developing regions, where external assistance for local self-help movements is less readily available. Such competition may make it difficult, in countries which are more popular with aid donors, for self-help movements to define their own strategies and maintain a balance between the mobilisation of people's own efforts and straight grant funding by aid. These situations may require a search for agreed approaches among NGOs of the North and between them and representative partner organisations over the next few years. A desirable outcome would also be a more balanced spread of NGO support across deprived areas in various countries both within Sub-Saharan Africa (where, for example, deprived areas in northern Togo are not as fashionable with donor NGOs as those in some other countries) and across major developing regions as well.

The search for ways to ensure core funding and ultimately self-sufficiency of host-country support institutions is likely to prove difficult. Donor sources could be more attentive to the core needs of structures which they expect to submit worthwhile projects for funding. Assistance to southern partners in the development of at least modest capitalised endowment funds is one possible solution recommended by experienced observers. Another suggestion, not necessarily an alternative, was mentioned at the DAC seminar held in June 1986: NGOs of the North could transfer the official contributions they receive to their partners in developing countries sooner than is current practice. The interest from funds in the period between receipt and expenditure would thus accrue to partners. There are few encouraging examples of such concern, but Danchurchaid already provides non-earmarked funds to partner African groups to finance their overhead costs. The experience quoted in Chapter IV of current support in Bangladesh by US AID for the small-business development society MIDAS, and by IFAD with Norway and Sweden for the Grameen Bank -- in both cases explicitly aimed at ensuring self-support within a few years -- may be worth following for possible replication elsewhere.

In the present context of inherently unequal relations between donor NGOs and their partners in the developing countries, there could be more of a search for possible forms of reciprocity. Examples were given in Chapter II. The Canadian NGO Inter Pares systematically seeks opportunities for reciprocity, making use of experience acquired by partners for activities in Canada, for example in adult education.

In their broader advocacy role within Member countries for more solidarity in interdependence, NGOs will probably increasingly need to develop an adequate analytical capacity. As already mentioned, suitable "think-tanks" exist in some DAC countries (and in a number of developing countries) in the form of independent research centres. Further efforts such as making existing capabilities more widely available and pooling professional skills to study complex issues will enhance the validity and impact of NGOs' assessments and their dialogue with governments in their own countries. There exist examples, such as, on the debt issue, the co-operation mentioned in Chapter VI between London's ODI and a British parliamentary group, or an ad hoc high-level research group established by ACFOA in Australia in preparation for the September 1987 World Bank-IMF meeting. Given the range of difficult developmental issues in which NGOs have become involved these co-operative approaches could usefully become a more frequent feature. Instances have occurred in which NGOs have documented undesirable environmental and poverty-extension effects of projects funded by the public sector, followed at times by corrective measures by the agencies concerned. Examples are provided by the EEC/NGO Liaison Committee, environmental and humanitarian associations in the United States, and the state-level Federation of Voluntary Organisations for Rural Development in the state of Karnataka, India.

Reciprocally, NGOs of the South need to increase their capacity for self-assessment and for appraising the forms of external support received. Expanded use of the techniques of self-evaluation developed with local organisations in Africa South of the Sahara and briefly outlined in Chapter III could be beneficial to this end, especially self-evaluations conducted together with representatives of the funding agencies. Co-operation can be improved by reciprocal criticism and opportunities for doing this should be greatly expanded, with support by the official aid agencies for the modest investment required.

The search for improved complementarities within broader development policies and programmes

The issue of impact and effectiveness is of growing importance for all agencies. In the case of NGOs, the issue is sharpened by the often limited and localised nature of their activities. The importance given in this report to support for local self-help organisations reflects the consensus of the DAC seminar held in June 1986 and is closely linked with the issue of impact. Several recent surveys quoted in previous chapters provide findings related to enhanced impact and these all clearly suggest the merit of more widespread reorientation of donor NGOs towards nurturing local organisations.

Support by "third generation" NGOs for the development of sustainable systems -- credit, health care, agricultural production and marketing -- within areas meaningful in terms of host-country jurisdiction and local planning, suggested by Dr. Korten's text on "micro-policy reform" mentioned in Chapter III, offers one path towards more sustained and better spread benefits, cost reduction and greater impact. Official aid agencies are themselves increasingly attentive to opportunities of this kind, for example through experimentation at district level of models for primary health care. Such developments in micro-policy reforms would help orient existing host-country systems and resources towards the needs of user populations and match them better with people's own contributions.

Closer consultation between donor NGOs and the public sector has great mutual value, as demonstrated by the interactive experience of the EEC-NGO Liaison Committee, the Commission of the European Communities and, increasingly, the European Parliament.

Developments in support for local partner institutions may also benefit from a common approach among donor NGOs, which may individually not have the capacity to respond to the various requirements of institution-building. This may be most meaningful within developing countries themselves and within an agreed in-country framework in assisting local self-help groups to develop and form their own associations, enacting co-ordination as a means to attain common goals of recognised priority.

Official donors can play a number of useful roles in co-operation with donor NGOs in a reorientation leaving more space to the initiative of partner organisations. As mentioned previously, they already contribute to a greater interest in host-country partners among NGOs of DAC countries by the procedures through which they extend cofinancing. More widespread use of non-earmarked funding and increased official aid for training and other invisible aspects of NGO operations in support of trustworthy intermediate institutions would help the promotion of self-help movements. The NORAD/ILO report on rural skills training in East Africa quoted in Chapter II exemplifies the need for such institutions.

Official donors also often perform a valuable "legitimising" role vis-à-vis the public sector in those host countries where NGOs and local self-help groups are a novelty, are viewed as competing for external funds or operate within an unfavourable environment. In a number of contexts where host-country public-sector services are inefficient and inadequately geared to the poor, official donors might be tempted to replace the needed dialogue with the host-country government by channelling more of their aid through NGOs.

This option would be ultimately self-defeating. It can also lead to an overburdening of existing local self-help organisations or deviation from their course, especially when they already fulfil functions which have a recognised priority over donors' particular offers. Official donors' role in the dialogue with host-country governments -- with its implications of in-depth knowledge of the problems or sectors under review, continuity, and availability of capable staff for an effective dialogue -- is irreplaceable. The dialogue at the governmental level can widen the impact of conclusions drawn from NGO activities and research and help to influence policies which favour the poor. More opportunities for institutionalised dialogue between aid agencies and the donor NGO sector within individual DAC countries would be an asset from this point of view. In many cases donor NGOs can document the impact of broader policies on the poor in developing countries. Institutionalised dialogue between NGOs internationally, and between NGOs and public-sector agencies, requires a modicum of resources to maintain a small permanent structure and make activities possible, as shown by the examples of ICVA, the EEC/NGO Liaison Committee and others. Foresight on the part of the public sector in providing these resources results in benefits in mutual understanding and improvements on both sides which, however difficult to quantify, are certainly out of proportion with the modest investments required.

An encouraging recent instance of a step from the other side -- that is, efforts by the public sector to involve domestic and external NGOs in policy consultations -- was provided by the technical meeting on cereals policies in Sahel countries organised by the CILSS (Inter-State Permanent Committee for Drought Control in the Sahel) and the Club du Sahel in Mindelo, Cape Verde, in December 1986 (5). NGO representatives including FONGS were invited there as observers for the first time. At the broader policy level, the symposium was concerned with the creation of more favourable conditions for increasing local production and regional trade in cereals, including more discerning use of food aid. With respect to local organisations, the final recommendations to governments of Sahel countries included:

-- Stimulating, encouraging and supporting producers' participatory structures aiming at identifying priority needs, and organising and managing operations favouring common interests such as agricultural credit, stocking of produce at village level, etc.;

-- Favouring the organisation of artisans in cereals processing and supporting informal-sector food trade, lifting legal constraints on petty food vendors in urban markets and streets, and encouraging local manufacturing of small-scale processing equipment.

Subsequent relevant activities included a series of studies by the Club du Sahel in 1987-88 on farmers' organisations in Burkina Faso, Mali, Senegal to assess their potential and identify their requirements to enhance their contribution to improvements in the rural areas (a consolidated report is expected in 1988). Prospects of the Sahel region for the year 2010 were studied jointly by the Secretariats of the Club du Sahel and the CILSS. The main conclusions as far as agriculture is concerned are that "instead of large-scale intervention by development agencies, it would be better to back up farmers' initiatives by responding to their demands, instead of seeking directly to create such initiatives. This approach presupposes the creation of peasant organisations and the definition of means of intervention designed to be close to the village communities and responsive to their requirements.

And the communities must be allowed more autonomy, which will in turn require contact with the political authorities" (6).

As noted by Dr. Korten, "first" or "second" generation NGOs will continue to be needed for many years to come. These provide relief from suffering, improve service delivery, help people to get organised to increase production, raise income or reduce their workload locally. At a different level, events such as the Mindelo meeting are an encouraging sign that "micro" and "macro" need not always work at cross-purposes, and that "third generation" institutions such as federations of farmers', villagers' and women's groups may come to participate in relevant policy formulation. There are many situations where change can be made less disruptive, the extension of poverty prevented, and living conditions improved by associating the people most directly affected in the search for solutions. In the complex and difficult business of development this is perhaps one of the areas where NGOs' role is the most valuable.

NOTES AND REFERENCES

1.   An important development was the creation in 1982 of the Global Committee of Parliamentarians on Population and Development, grouping majority and opposition parliamentarians from about 60 countries, both developed and developing, and working as a liaison body.

2.   Backstopping in the case of environmental concerns is provided by the International Institute for Environment and Development and its activities in policy research, information and field activities to promote sustainable development programmes. Founded in 1971 as a non-profit organisation, funded by governmental and intergovernmental agencies and foundations, NGOs, and corporations, with a budget of $3.7 million in 1986 and offices in London, Washington and Buenos Aires, IIED acts in particular with the media, bilateral and multilateral development co-operation agencies, research institutions in developing countries, and NGOs. See IIED's annual reports.

3.   These issues are thoughtfully considered in the concluding chapters of David Millwood and Helena Gezelius, Good Aid, A Study of Quality in Small Projects, 246 pp., SIDA, Stockholm, 1985.

4.   ACFOA, Development in the Pacific: What Women Say, Development Dossier No. 18, Canberra, 1986.

5.   CILSS, Club du Sahel, Les politiques céréalières dans les pays du Sahel, Actes du Colloque de Mindelo, Paris, 1987.

6.   Anne de Lattre, "What Future for the Sahel?" in The OECD Observer, No 153, August-September 1988, which discusses the mains issues of The Sahel Facing the Future: Increasing Dependence or Structural Transformation. Futures Study of the Sahel Countries 1985-2010, OECD, forthcoming autumn 1988, a study prepared by a team of consultants led by Jacques Giri.

LIST OF ABBREVIATIONS

ACFOA   Australian Council for Overseas Aid (national NGO council)

ACORD   Agency for Co-operation and Research in Development (formerly EURO-ACTION ACORD)

ACVAFS   American Council of Voluntary Agencies for Foreign Service (replaced by INTERACTION)

AID   Agency for International Development (official aid agency of the United States, also designated as US AID)

ASSEFA   Association of Sarva Seva Farms (India)

BRAC   Bangladesh Rural Advancement Committee

CAFOD   Catholic Fund for Overseas Development (British NGO)

CARE   Co-operative for American Relief Everywhere

CCFD   Comité catholique contre la faim et pour le développement (French NGO)

CCIC   Canadian Council for International Co-operation (national NGO council)

CEBEMO   Catholic Organisation for the Joint Financing of Development Programmes (Dutch NGO "umbrella" organisation)

CEC   Commission of the European Communities

CESAO   Centre d'études économiques et sociales en Afrique de l'Ouest

CFCF   Comité français contre la faim (French freedom from hunger committee)

CIDA   Canadian International Development Agency (Canada's official aid agency)

CONGAD   Conseil des ONG d'appui au développement (Senegal)

COPAC   Committee for the Promotion of Aid to Co-operatives

DAI	Development Alternatives Inc. (US PVO)
DANIDA	Danish International Development Agency (Denmark's official development co-operation agency)
Deutsche Welthungerhilfe	German Freedom from Hunger NGO
ECAD	European Consortium for Agricultural Development (grouping several European NGOs; CFCF, Deutsche Welthungerhilfe, Mani Tese, NOVIB and the Belgian SOS-Faim)
ECU	Unit of account of the European Communities
EZE	Evangelische Zentralstelle für Entwicklungshilfe (German Protestant developmental NGO)
FINNIDA	Finnish International Development Agency (Finland's official development co-operation agency)
FOCSIV	Federation of Catholic Organisations for International Voluntary Service (Italian NGO "umbrella" organisation)
FONGS	Fédération des ONG du Sénégal (national small-farmers' movement)
HIVOS	Humanist Institute for Co-operation with Developing Countries (Dutch NGO "umbrella" organisation)
ICCO	Dutch "umbrella" organisation of Protestant developmental NGOs
ICVA	International Council of Voluntary Agencies
IFAD	International Fund for Agricultural Development
IIED	International Institute for Environment and Development
INADES	Institut africain pour le développement économique et social
INTERACTION	"Umbrella" organisation of US developmental NGOs
IRED	Innovation et réseaux pour le développement (South-South NGO network, Geneva)
ODC	Overseas Development Council (Washington)
ODI	Overseas Development Institute (London)
ORAP	Organisation of Rural Associations for Progress (Zimbabwe)
PVO	Private Voluntary Organisation
MIDAS	Micro-Industries Development and Assistance Society (Bangladesh)
MISEREOR	Developmental and relief agency of German Catholic bishops

NAAM	Traditional youth associations of the Mossi people in the Yatenga region and name of a villagers' movement (Burkina Faso)
NORAD	Norwegian Agency for International Development (Norway's official development co-operation agency)
NOVIB	Netherlands Organisation for International Development Co-operation ("umbrella" organisation of Dutch non-denominational developmental NGOs)
PACT	Private Agencies Collaborating Together (a consortium of US PVOs)
RONGEAD	Réseau des ONG européennes sur les questions agro-alimentaires et le développement [European NGOs' network on agriculture, food and development (ENAFOOD)]
SEWA	Self-Employed Women's Association (India)
SIDA	Swedish International Development Authority (Sweden's official development co-operation agency)
"Six S"	"Se servir de la saison sèche en savanne et au Sahel" (international NGO supporting self-help movements in West Africa)
SOLAGRAL	Solidarités agricoles et alimentaires (French NGO, affiliate of RONGEAD/ENAFOOD)
TAICH	Technical Assistance Information Clearing House of ACVAFS (no longer operating)
TROCAIRE	Irish Catholic developmental NGO
UN-NGLS	United Nations Non-governmental Liaison Service
WOCCU	World Council of Credit Unions

Annex 2

NGO STATEMENT SUBMITTED TO THE 509TH MEETING OF
THE DEVELOPMENT ASSISTANCE COMMITTEE
(3rd-4th June 1986)

The representatives of African, Northern and International NGOs submit this joint statement to the OECD Development Assistance Committee seminar on the role of NGOs in agricultural and rural development in Sub-Saharan Africa.

1.   We recognise that the development of Sub-Saharan Africa is the responsibility of Africans themselves and that African NGOs, including formal and informal community groups, have an essential role in this process. We further wish to emphasize the need to integrate African women fully in the development process, and call for applied research by Africans and others on the African socio-cultural experience.

2.   In our opinion the principal roles to be played by Northern NGOs are:

    i) To endeavour to seek changes in Northern economic and development policies through advocacy, development education and building public awareness so as to ensure that these policies are conducive to sustainable development in Africa;

    ii) To provide support -- financial, training, technical assistance, management -- when requested by African NGOs while fully respecting their autonomy; and,

    iii) To encourage the development of African NGOs.

3.   NGOs recognise their role as complementary to governments in the development process and consequently wish to act in partnership with them.

4.   We believe that the prerequisite for dynamic development in Sub-Saharan Africa is the strengthening of African NGO capacities and therefore urge support for:

    i) Involving NGOs from the initial stages in development programmes;

    ii) Institution building of African NGOs;

    iii) Exchanging information among African NGOs;

    iv) Establishing and strengthening African NGO councils and networks;

    v) Creating direct funding mechanisms for African national NGOs; and,

vi) Covering the costs of appraising and evaluating NGO projects.

NGOs view these proposals as an essential part of the process of agricultural and rural development in Sub-Saharan Africa.

Annex 3

INSTITUTIONAL DEVELOPMENT CATEGORIES AND INDICATORS
OF INDIGENOUS ORGANISATIONS (IO)
(DAI-Cornell)

A. Internal capacity building categories

1. Resource management (allocation, distribution and mediation)

   a) IO possesses and maintains adequate financial resources, facilities and equipment.

   b) Resources are allocated according to predetermined and established criteria.

   c) Resources are distributed efficiently and in a timely fashion.

   d) System(s) exists for mediation in conflicts over distribution of resources.

2. Service delivery

   a) Services or products in type and quality meet needs of beneficiaries and clients.

   b) Supply is distributed efficiently.

3. Diversification (ability to innovate and be flexible)

   a) Programmes/solutions have been undertaken to meet additional beneficiary demands.

   b) Diversification has not over-extended the IO.

   c) Expansion of service delivery has not over-extended the IO.

4. Human resources, administrative performance/incentives

   a) IO has adequate number of staff to perform key functions.

   b) Appropriate incentives exist to motivate staff.

c) IO has authority to hire, fire, remunerate staff.

d) IO has regular (formal, informal) training programme for staff.

5. <u>Leadership and management style</u>

a) Ways of leader selection seen as legitimate by staff/members.

b) Decisions are taken on the basis of consultation.

c) Divisions of responsibility reflect IO's tasks and competences and are clearly understood by IO staff.

6. <u>Planning, monitoring and evaluation</u>

a) There is a planning process that is documented, perceived as useful, and utilised by IO.

b) Information is gathered and records are kept that permit assessment of progress toward meeting objectives (expenses, activities, performance, outputs, problems).

c) Evaluations have been used to assist in the planning process.

7. <u>Learning</u>

a) IO has made deliberate modifications of its objectives and programmes on the basis of experience/evidence.

b) Evidence of regular interchange of information among IO staff, with constituency groups, and interested organisations.

B. <u>External legitimacy building categories</u>

8. <u>Forging links</u> (horizontal and vertical)

a) IO has entered into formal/informal agreements to exchange services, resources or information.

b) IO has received official recognition from public, private, or international authorities.

9. <u>Claim-making</u> (leverage and advocacy)

a) IO represents interests of its constituency with the government, local elites, and other authorities.

b) IO able to mobilise resources required/desired by its constituency from other sources.

C. Categories common to internal capacity building and external legitimacy building

    10. Resource mobilisation/income generation

        a) IO has access to resources required to do the job.

        b) IO has control over resources.

        c) IO has specific awareness of future resources needed and realistic idea of where they will come from.

        d) IO mobilises resources from its members/constituency.

    11. Accountability/responsiveness

        a) Specific procedures exist for client group input and influence over 10.

        b. IO has satisfactorily responded to client group demands.

        c. IO accounts to constituency for their financial participation.

    12. Conflict management (resolution/mediation)

        a) IO mediates conflicting interests among constituency or members.

    13. Demonstration Effect

        a) IO has served as a model for replication.

Ratings may be: Not applicable
                  Very Low
                  Adequate
                  Well

Source: Development Alternatives Inc., study on IVS and IIDI under contract with US AID, 1984. Full reference in Chapter III.

STATISTICAL ANNEX

List of tables

Table 1. PRIVATE GRANTS BY VOLUNTARY AGENCIES, 1970-79
US$ million equivalent

	1970	1971	1972	1973	1974	1975	1976	1977	1978	1979
Australia	15.7	18.7	17.4	22.0	37.4	33.8	37.2	35.9	38.3	49.2
Austria	3.6	4.1	4.6	8.9	9.6	11.1	11.0	10.8	14.6	16.1
Belgium	14.8	12.0	12.0	15.0	17.5	20.0	22.5	27.3	31.5	41.0
Canada	51.6	49.0	54.0	78.4	56.5	66.5	106.0	103.0	87.0	96.0
Denmark	3.0	4.4	5.7	5.9	5.3	6.2	5.6	6.6	8.1	10.4
Finland	0.8	0.8	1.0	1.3	1.8	2.2	4.5	4.9	6.2	10.1
France	6.3	7.2	7.9	10.0	12.5	15.2	15.1	16.3	19.9	23.5
Germany	77.8	108.3	123.6	157.2	177.4	205.0	204.6	225.0	284.0	389.4
Ireland	-	-	-	-	-	-	-	-	-	-
Italy	5.0	6.0	10.3	21.0	1.9	3.0	0.2	1.1	0.3	0.2
Japan	2.9	3.1	5.6	6.8	8.7	10.1	16.2	18.3	18.9	19.0
Netherlands	5.2	10.0	15.0	15.0	19.5	23.5	30.5	42.7	55.5	65.3
New Zealand	1.4	1.7	4.8	5.1	5.8	6.4	5.5	5.6	5.9	9.6
Norway	3.9	5.3	7.9	6.9	11.8	10.6	19.2	23.5	25.9	30.0
Sweden	25.2	23.6	27.2	29.9	32.9	38.8	43.4	43.5	44.3	49.0
Switzerland	10.9	14.2	19.7	19.9	27.6	32.1	34.4	34.4	48.6	51.3
United Kingdom	33.6	46.2	50.0	56.4	56.1	57.8	52.4	50.0	55.7	107.7
United States	598.0	599.0	669.0	905.0	735.0	804.0	789.0	840.0	931.0	1 029.0
Total DAC countries	859.6	913.6	1 035.7	1 364.6	1 217.3	1 346.3	1 397.2	1 488.7	1 675.4	1 996.8
Total DAC countries at 1986 prices and exchange rates	2 728.9	2 690.2	2 740.7	3 129.8	2 548.3	2 438.9	2 459.0	2 405.8	2 326.3	2 502.9

Table 2. PRIVATE GRANTS BY VOLUNTARY AGENCIES, 1980-86
US$ million equivalent

	1980	1981	1982	1983	1984	1985	1986
Australia	39.8	35.8	33.5	32.2	40.8	52.1	39.5
Austria	23.5	20.2	15.3	12.2	12.5	18.5	19.4
Belgium	45.0	37.3	31.8	3.9	15.6	22.7	23.0
Canada	102.0	103.0	123.0	132.0	141.0	171.0	176.0
Denmark	12.9	10.0	9.3	13.0	11.9	15.6	12.2
Finland	15.5	13.4	14.3	16.2	18.5	12.7	27.6
France	35.7	32.0	30.4	36.0	34.0	64.8	84.0
Germany	420.7	371.1	390.8	370.4	382.4	423.8	544.7
Ireland	..	..	..	..	21.2	22.4	20.2
Italy	3.1	1.2	3.3	3.3	8.4	8.1	10.8
Japan	26.4	27.3	23.3	29.7	40.7	101.4	81.6
Netherlands	78.7	85.2	107.9	107.2	100.8	97.7	139.9
New Zealand	6.8	6.8	6.7	6.8	6.9	8.2	6.7
Norway	33.0	36.0	38.9	42.8	47.1	51.8	57.0
Sweden	59.0	59.0	60.0	61.0	62.0	77.6	85.3
Switzerland	63.2	53.8	48.5	48.0	49.9	53.9	66.4
United Kingdom	120.2	95.3	99.8	83.4	140.3	168.5	190.6
United States	1 301.0	1 018.0	1 280.0	1 320.0	1 464.0	1 513.0	1 753.0
Total DAC countries	2 386.3	2 005.3	2 316.8	2 318.1	2 598.0	2 883.7	3 337.8
Total DAC countries at 1986 prices and exchange rates	2 730.6	2 379.9	2 806.5	2 815.6	3 223.3	3 540.0	3 337.8

Table 3. OFFICIAL CONTRIBUTIONS TO NATIONAL PRIVATE VOLUNTARY AGENCIES, 1970-79
$ million

	1970	1971	1972	1973	1974	1975	1976	1977	1978	1979
Australia	-	-	..	0.2	0.1	0.6	0.9	1.3	1.8	2.2
Austria	0.6	0.5	0.8	..	8.1	9.7	11.4	25.1	33.7	..
Belgium	..	5.6	7.8	7.6	9.0	9.7	10.0	20.6	25.9	35.8
Canada	..	11.0	7.3	12.6	24.5	31.5	33.5	33.4	53.3	54.7
Denmark	..	..	..	..	..	..	..	3.0	..	..
Finland	-	-	-	-	..	..	0.1	0.3	0.6	..
France	..	..	..	..	-	..	..	5.1	5.1	..
Germany	..	..	..	..	..	..	43.7	49.0	60.2	(100.0)
Ireland	..	..	..	..	..	..	..	..	..	..
Italy	..	..	..	..	-	..	..	..	..	..
Japan	..	6.0	5.4	0.4	8.4	9.8	11.7	14.5	24.2	22.6
Netherlands	..	..	..	..	19.4	21.5	47.7	54.2	60.6	82.7
New Zealand	-	-	0.2	0.2	0.2	0.2	0.2	0.8	0.3	0.8
Norway	1.0	1.1	1.1	1.4	4.7	9.3	6.5	6.2	7.6	8.8
Sweden	8.8	8.1	7.5	9.5	5.4	10.0	13.3	19.6	27.9	36.2
Switzerland	2.5	1.5	2.7	5.5	4.6	5.0	7.4	7.9	18.1	19.4
United Kingdom	..	2.9	3.5	3.7	4.4	4.0	4.7	6.3	9.3	13.7
United States	..	..	..	..	..	..	325.0	486.9	485.0	(500.0)
Total DAC countries	12.9	36.8	36.2	41.0	88.8	111.3	516.1	734.3	813.6	(876.9)
Total DAC countries at 1986 prices and exchange rates	40.9	108.4	95.8	94.0	185.9	201.6	908.3	1 186.7	1 129.7	(1 099.2)
EEC (a)	-	-	-	-	-	-	2.8	4.5	15.4	(15.4)

( ) = Secretariat estimates.   a. Matching grants only, excluding food and emergency aid.

Table 4. OFFICIAL CONTRIBUTIONS TO NATIONAL PRIVATE VOLUNTARY AGENCIES, 1980-86
$ million

	1980	1981	1982	1983	1984	1985	1986
Australia	5.7	6.2	10.2	10.4	18.2	12.8	5.0
Austria	..	..	..	..	..	1.0	1.7
Belgium	38.2	30.9	21.6	15.7	14.4	27.4	35.6
Canada	12.2	70.0	103.9	124.7	147.1	128.6	167.6
Denmark	..	12.7	16.8	18.3	10.6	6.9	..
Finland	1.4	1.8	1.9	2.1	4.1	4.1	7.6
France	3.5	16.0	16.3	14.2	..	42.5	17.3
Germany	198.4	175.9	169.7	177.1	174.7	174.0	248.0
Ireland	-	-	-	-	1.6	1.9	3.5
Italy	..	2.3	..	..	-	39.1	42.1
Japan	26.9	28.7	27.7	30.5	37.3	41.3	91.7
Netherlands	87.8	85.9	97.1	86.6	81.5	68.9	112.4
New Zealand	1.0	1.2	1.0	1.4	0.9	0.7	0.7
Norway	12.3	14.0	28.6	24.0	26.3	34.1	49.8
Sweden	49.2	50.0	49.3	28.9	36.0	33.0	36.8
Switzerland	..	33.8	42.2	49.5	45.6	40.6	59.4
United Kingdom	3.5	6.0	4.6	4.3	6.5	13.2	11.8
United States	604.7	717.9	568.2	595.2	718.7	802.8	1 060.0
Total DAC countries	1 044.6	1 253.2	1 159.2	1 182.9	1 323.5	1 472.9	1 951.0
Total DAC countries at 1986 prices and exchange rates	1 195.3	1 487.3	1 404.2	1 436.8	1 642.1	1 808.1	1 951.0
EEC (a)	19.5	15.7	26.3	23.1	27.6	29.4	48.7

a. Matching grants only (including, in addition to the cofinancing of projects, $2.7 million for public awareness in 1985 and $4.4 million in 1986) excluding food and emergency aid.

Table 5. OFFICIAL CONTRIBUTIONS TO INTERNATIONAL PRIVATE AGENCIES AND TOTAL OFFICIAL CONTRIBUTIONS TO NATIONAL AND INTERNATIONAL PRIVATE AGENCIES AS A PERCENTAGE OF TOTAL ODA, 1985-86

	1985			1986		
	Official contributions to international NGOs	Total official contributions to national and international NGOs	As a percentage of total ODA	Official contributions to international NGOs	Total official contributions to national and international NGOs	As a percentage of total ODA
	US$ million	US$ million	%	US$ million	US$ million	%
Australia	0	13	1.7	1	6	0.8
Austria	..	1	0.4	..	2	1.0
Belgium	0	27	6.1	0	36	6.6
Canada	13	142	8.7	15	183	10.8
Denmark	..	7	1.6	..	..	..
Finland	1	5	2.4	1	9	2.9
France	..	43	1.1	0	17	0.3
Germany	..	174	5.9	..	248	6.5
Ireland	..	2	5.1	..	3	4.8
Italy	2	41	3.7	3	45	1.9
Japan	1	42	1.1	1	92	1.6
Netherlands	2	71	6.3	10	122	7.0
New Zealand	0	1	1.9	0	1	1.3
Norway	..	34	5.9	0	49	6.1
Sweden	8	41	4.9	13	50	4.6
Switzerland	11	52	17.2	23	82	19.4
United Kingdom	14	27	1.8	11	23	1.3
United States	..	803	8.5	..	1 060	11.1

Table 6. PRIVATE GRANTS BY VOLUNTARY AGENCIES AS A PERCENTAGE OF GNP, 1975, 1980, 1985, 1986

	1975		1980		1985		1986	
	US$ million equivalent	% of GNP	US$ million equivalent	% of GNP	US$ million equivalent	% of GNP	US$ million equivalent	% of GNP
Australia	34	0.04	40	0.03	52	0.03	40	0.02
Austria	11	0.03	24	0.03	18	0.03	19	0.02
Belgium	20	0.03	45	0.04	23	0.03	23	0.02
Canada	67	0.04	102	0.04	171	0.05	176	0.05
Denmark	6	0.02	13	0.02	16	0.03	12	0.02
Finland	2	0.01	16	0.03	13	0.02	28	0.04
France	15	0.00	36	0.01	65	0.01	84	0.01
Germany	205	0.05	421	0.05	424	0.07	545	0.06
Ireland	-	-	-	-	22	0.14	20	0.09
Italy	3	0.00	3	0.00	8	0.00	11	0.00
Japan	10	0.00	26	0.00	101	0.01	82	0.00
Netherlands	24	0.03	79	0.05	98	0.08	140	0.08
New Zealand	6	0.05	7	0.03	8	0.04	7	0.03
Norway	11	0.04	33	0.06	52	0.09	57	0.08
Sweden	39	0.05	59	0.05	78	0.08	85	0.07
Switzerland	32	0.06	63	0.06	54	0.06	66	0.05
United Kingdom	58	0.03	120	0.02	169	0.04	191	0.03
United States	804	0.05	1 301	0.05	1 513	0.04	1 753	0.04
Total DAC countries	1 346	0.03	2 386	0.03	2 884	0.03	3 338	0.03

Table 7. VOLUNTEERS SERVING OVERSEAS WHOLLY OR PARTLY FINANCED BY OFFICIAL AID AGENCIES, 1975, 1980, 1985-86
Number of persons and official expenditures

	Number of persons				US$ million			
	1975	1980	1985	1986	1975	1980	1985	1986
Australia	157	126	249	257	0.1	0.3	1.7	1.5
Austria	276	251	267	260	1.3	2.8	2.8	3.5
Belgium	657	933	1 461	(1 461)	2.2	5.5	6.2	(6.2)
Canada	1 195	1 263	2 354	2 422	10.3	18.0	24.2	20.3
Denmark	401	380	465	(465)	2.8	..	7.4	(7.4)
Finland	0	7	12	13	0	0.1	0.1	(0.1)
France	(2 100)	(2 100)	(2 100)	2 100	..	(50.0)	67.4	98.3
Germany	1 720	(1 650)	1 597	1 725	13.7	44.6	42.3	58.6
Ireland	-	-	575	575	-	-	..	1.8
Italy	504	719	895	1 010	1.9	..	16.0	23.2
Japan	712	1 076	2 073	2 434	4.1	11.1	23.0	35.4
Netherlands	687	597	625	582	9.0	15.3	12.7	17.8
New Zealand	(90)	98	89	89	1.1	0.2	0.3	0.5
Norway	114	125	213	204	1.6	..	6.3	6.4
Sweden	182	58	(58)	(58)		1.1	..	..
Switzerland	117	357	(357)	(357)	0.9	2.4	(2.4)	(2.4)
United Kingdom	1 915	1 103	1 636	1 745	2.1	31.5	8.9	9.2
United States	(5 000)	5 194	4 349	5 132	(50.0)	76.2	90.8	96.6
Total DAC countries	8 637	12 287	16 285	18 548	51.1	289.1	310.1	373.1
Including estimates	(15 827)	(16 037)	(18 800)	(20 889)	(101.1)	(259.1)	(312.5)	(389.2)

( ) Secretariat estimates.

Table 8. COMPOSITION OF OFFICIAL CONTRIBUTIONS TO NATIONAL PRIVATE VOLUNTARY AGENCIES
FROM SELECTED DAC MEMBERS, 1983
US$ million

	Australia	Denmark	France	Germany	Netherlands	Sweden	United States	EEC
Food aid and relief	6.03	4.82	-	10.18	18.57	14.68	324.30	57.86
Regular food aid	-	-	-	(4.11	9.81	-	(319.20	(46.29
Emergency relief food aid	3.18	-	-	(..	-	1.62	(..	(..
Other relief commodities	-	-	-	3.68	-	0.14	4.10	11.57
Emergency relief cash contributions	2.85	4.82	-	2.39	8.76	12.92	1.00	-
Cash contributions	12.13	13.50	12.49	166.91	88.99	28.99	239.40	23.06
Regular programmes	12.13	9.68	3.31	165.15	88.99	26.75	214.50	21.10
Other	-	3.82	9.18(a)	1.76	-	2.24	24.90(b)	1.96(c)
Contributions to LDC-NGOs	-	-	1.71	-	3.68	0.44	31.50	-
Total	18.16	18.32	14.20	177.09	111.24	44.11	595.20	80.92

a.   Association française Volontaires du progrès.
b.   Ocean freight reimbursement $7.5 million; refugee assistance $17.4 million.
c.   Development education.

WHERE TO OBTAIN OECD PUBLICATIONS
OÙ OBTENIR LES PUBLICATIONS DE L'OCDE

ARGENTINA - ARGENTINE
Carlos Hirsch S.R.L.,
Florida 165, 4º Piso,
(Galeria Guemes) 1333 Buenos Aires
Tel. 33.1787.2391 y 30.7122

AUSTRALIA - AUSTRALIE
D.A. Book (Aust.) Pty. Ltd.
11-13 Station Street (P.O. Box 163)
Mitcham, Vic. 3132   Tel. (03) 873 4411

AUSTRIA - AUTRICHE
OECD Publications and Information Centre,
4 Simrockstrasse,
5300 Bonn (Germany)   Tel. (0228) 21.60.45
Gerold & Co., Graben 31, Wien 1   Tel. 52.22.35

BELGIUM - BELGIQUE
Jean de Lannoy,
Avenue du Roi 202
B-1060 Bruxelles   Tel. (02) 538.51.69

CANADA
Renouf Publishing Company Ltd/
Éditions Renouf Ltée,
1294 Algoma Road, Ottawa, Ont. K1B 3W8
Tel: (613) 741-4333
Toll Free/Sans Frais:
Ontario, Quebec, Maritimes:
1-800-267-1805
Western Canada, Newfoundland:
1-800-267-1826
Stores/Magasins:
61 rue Sparks St., Ottawa, Ont. K1P 5A6
Tel: (613) 238-8985
211 rue Yonge St., Toronto, Ont. M5B 1M4
Tel: (416) 363-3171
Federal Publications Inc.,
301-303 King St. W.,
Toronto, Ont. M5V 1J5
Tel. (416)581-1552
Les Éditions la Liberté inc.,
3020 Chemin Sainte-Foy,
Sainte-Foy, P.Q. G1X 3V6,
Tel. (418)658-3763

DENMARK - DANEMARK
Munksgaard Export and Subscription Service
35, Nørre Søgade, DK-1370 København K
Tel. +45.1.12.85.70

FINLAND - FINLANDE
Akateeminen Kirjakauppa,
Keskuskatu 1, 00100 Helsinki 10   Tel. 0.12141

FRANCE
OCDE/OECD
Mail Orders/Commandes par correspondance :
2, rue André-Pascal,
75775 Paris Cedex 16
Tel. (1) 45.24.82.00
Bookshop/Librairie : 33, rue Octave-Feuillet
75016 Paris
Tel. (1) 45.24.81.67 or/ou (1) 45.24.81.81
Librairie de l'Université,
12a, rue Nazareth,
13602 Aix-en-Provence   Tel. 42.26.18.08

GERMANY - ALLEMAGNE
OECD Publications and Information Centre,
4 Simrockstrasse,
5300 Bonn   Tel. (0228) 21.60.45

GREECE - GRÈCE
Librairie Kauffmann,
28, rue du Stade, 105 64 Athens   Tel. 322.21.60

HONG KONG
Government Information Services,
Publications (Sales) Office,
Information Services Department
No. 1, Battery Path, Central

ICELAND - ISLANDE
Snæbjörn Jónsson & Co., h.f.,
Hafnarstræti 4 & 9,
P.O.B. 1131 - Reykjavik
Tel. 13133/14281/11936

INDIA - INDE
Oxford Book and Stationery Co.,
Scindia House, New Delhi 110001
Tel. 331.5896/5308
17 Park St., Calcutta 700016   Tel. 240832

INDONESIA - INDONÉSIE
Pdii-Lipi, P.O. Box 3065/JKT.Jakarta
Tel. 583467

IRELAND - IRLANDE
TDC Publishers - Library Suppliers,
12 North Frederick Street, Dublin 1
Tel. 744835-749677

ITALY - ITALIE
Libreria Commissionaria Sansoni,
Via Lamarmora 45, 50121 Firenze
Tel. 579751/584468
Via Bartolini 29, 20155 Milano   Tel. 365083
La diffusione delle pubblicazioni OCSE viene
assicurata dalle principali librerie ed anche da :
Editrice e Libreria Herder,
Piazza Montecitorio 120, 00186 Roma
Tel. 6794628
Libreria Hœpli,
Via Hœpli 5, 20121 Milano   Tel. 865446
Libreria Scientifica
Dott. Lucio de Biasio "Aeiou"
Via Meravigli 16, 20123 Milano   Tel. 807679

JAPAN - JAPON
OECD Publications and Information Centre,
Landic Akasaka Bldg., 2-3-4 Akasaka,
Minato-ku, Tokyo 107   Tel. 586.2016

KOREA - CORÉE
Kyobo Book Centre Co. Ltd.
P.O.Box: Kwang Hwa Moon 1658,
Seoul   Tel. (REP) 730.78.91

LEBANON - LIBAN
Documenta Scientifica/Redico,
Edison Building, Bliss St.,
P.O.B. 5641, Beirut   Tel. 354429-344425

MALAYSIA/SINGAPORE -
MALAISIE/SINGAPOUR
University of Malaya Co-operative Bookshop
Ltd.,
7 Lrg 51A/227A, Petaling Jaya
Malaysia   Tel. 7565000/7565425
Information Publications Pte Ltd
Pei-Fu Industrial Building,
24 New Industrial Road No. 02-06
Singapore 1953   Tel. 2831786, 2831798

NETHERLANDS - PAYS-BAS
SDU Uitgeverij
Christoffel Plantijnstraat 2
Postbus 20014
2500 EA's-Gravenhage   Tel. 070-789911
Voor bestellingen: Tel. 070-789880

NEW ZEALAND - NOUVELLE-ZÉLANDE
Government Printing Office Bookshops:
Auckland: Retail Bookshop, 25 Rutland Stseet,
Mail Orders, 85 Beach Road
Private Bag C.P.O.
Hamilton: Retail: Ward Street,
Mail Orders, P.O. Box 857
Wellington: Retail, Mulgrave Street, (Head
Office)
Cubacade World Trade Centre,
Mail Orders, Private Bag
Christchurch: Retail, 159 Hereford Street,
Mail Orders, Private Bag
Dunedin: Retail, Princes Street,
Mail Orders, P.O. Box 1104

NORWAY - NORVÈGE
Narvesen Info Center - NIC,
Bertrand Narvesens vei 2,
P.O.B. 6125 Etterstad, 0602 Oslo 6
Tel. (02) 67.83.10, (02) 68.40.20

PAKISTAN
Mirza Book Agency
65 Shahrah Quaid-E-Azam, Lahore 3 Tel. 66839

PHILIPPINES
I.J. Sagun Enterprises, Inc.
P.O. Box 4322 CPO Manila
Tel. 695-1946, 922-9495

PORTUGAL
Livraria Portugal,
Rua do Carmo 70-74,
1117 Lisboa Codex   Tel. 360582/3

SINGAPORE/MALAYSIA -
SINGAPOUR/MALAISIE
See "Malaysia/Singapor". Voir
« Malaisie/Singapour »

SPAIN - ESPAGNE
Mundi-Prensa Libros, S.A.,
Castelló 37, Apartado 1223, Madrid-28001
Tel. 431.33.99
Libreria Bosch, Ronda Universidad 11,
Barcelona 7   Tel. 317.53.08/317.53.58

SWEDEN - SUÈDE
AB CE Fritzes Kungl. Hovbokhandel,
Box 16356, S 103 27 STH,
Regeringsgatan 12,
DS Stockholm   Tel. (08) 23.89.00
Subscription Agency/Abonnements:
Wennergren-Williams AB,
Box 30004, S104 25 Stockholm Tel. (08)54.12.00

SWITZERLAND - SUISSE
OECD Publications and Information Centre,
4 Simrockstrasse,
5300 Bonn (Germany)   Tel. (0228) 21.60.45
Librairie Payot,
6 rue Grenus, 1211 Genève 11
Tel. (022) 31.89.50
United Nations Bookshop/Librairie des Nations-
Unies
Palais des Nations,
1211 – Geneva 10
Tel. 022-34-60-11 (ext. 48 72)

TAIWAN - FORMOSE
Good Faith Worldwide Int'l Co., Ltd.
9th floor, No. 118, Sec.2
Chung Hsiao E. Road
Taipei   Tel. 391.7396/391.7397

THAILAND - THAILANDE
Suksit Siam Co., Ltd., 1715 Rama IV Rd.,
Samyam Bangkok 5   Tel. 2511630
INDEX Book Promotion & Service Ltd.
59/6 Soi Lang Suan, Ploenchit Road
Patjumamwan, Bangkok 10500
Tel. 250-1919, 252-1066

TURKEY - TURQUIE
Kültur Yayinlari Is-Türk Ltd. Sti.
Atatürk Bulvari No: 191/Kat. 21
Kavaklidere/Ankara   Tel. 25.07.60
Dolmabahce Cad. No: 29
Besiktas/Istanbul   Tel. 160.71.88

UNITED KINGDOM - ROYAUME-UNI
H.M. Stationery Office,
Postal orders only: (01)211-5656
P.O.B. 276, London SW8 5DT
Telephone orders: (01) 622.3316, or
Personal callers:
49 High Holborn, London WC1V 6HB
Branches at: Belfast, Birmingham,
Bristol, Edinburgh, Manchester

UNITED STATES - ÉTATS-UNIS
OECD Publications and Information Centre,
2001 L Street, N.W., Suite 700,
Washington, D.C. 20036 - 4095
Tel. (202) 785.6323

VENEZUELA
Libreria del Este,
Avda F. Miranda 52, Aptdo. 60337,
Edificio Galipan, Caracas 106
Tel. 951.17.05/951.23.07/951.12.97

YUGOSLAVIA - YOUGOSLAVIE
Jugoslovenska Knjiga, Knez Mihajlova 2,
P.O.B. 36, Beograd   Tel. 621.992

Orders and inquiries from countries where
Distributors have not yet been appointed should be
sent to:
OECD, Publications Service, 2, rue André-Pascal,
75775 PARIS CEDEX 16.

Les commandes provenant de pays où l'OCDE n'a
pas encore désigné de distributeur doivent être
adressées à :
OCDE, Service des Publications. 2, rue André-
Pascal, 75775 PARIS CEDEX 16.

71784-07-1988

OECD PUBLICATIONS, 2, rue André-Pascal, 75775 PARIS CEDEX 16 - No. 44537 1988
PRINTED IN FRANCE
(43 88 05 1)   ISBN 92-64-13153-1